EAGLE
America's Sailing Square-Rigger

EAGLE
America's Sailing Square-Rigger

George Putz

The Globe Pequot Press

Chester, Connecticut 06412

The publisher gratefully acknowledges the use of color photographs from the U.S. Coast Guard taken by Doug Bandos except: cadet in shorts climbing the rigging taken by Neil Ruenzel and photo of Coast Guard Slash from Coast Guard archives.

Manufactured in the
United States of America

First Edition/First Printing

Library of Congress Càtaloging-in-Publication Data

Putz, George.
    Eagle, America's sailing square-rigger.

    Includes index.
    1. Eagle (Ship).   I. Title.
VG53.P87 1986   387.2′2   86-7632
ISBN 0-87106-897-4 (pbk.)
ISBN 0-87106-826-5

Contents

This book is dedicated to Erik Alexandre Putz and Jessica Hoyt Putz, my children, who as they enter their majority I admonish to continue to seek and cherish the voyages of friendship they have so lovingly lavished on me. Sail, kids, and may the wind be on your quarter, most of your times.

Many thanks must be tendered to the people who have helped and supported this project. Among the principals, certainly Captain Ernst Cummings, commanding officer of *Eagle*, reigns. His consummate leadership, advice and knowledge, and friendship have infused this work from the beginning. And, too, Chief Warrant Officer Richard Shannon, *Eagle*'s sail master, has also made help and friendship one thing.

Paul Johnson, Coast Guard Academy historian, has been an abiding presence—not only helpful, but always reminding one of standards. Lt. Neil Ruenzel, now in civilian life, and his successor, Lt. Paul Preusse, both of the Coast Guard Academy's Office of Public Affairs, were always gracious and generous with their initiative, enthusiasm, and resources. Certainly, CPO Doug Bandos of the Public Affairs Office must be thanked, not only for much service but also for superb judgment and skill in providing photographic resources, discernment, and editing.

Robert Scheina, United States Coast Guard historian at the service headquarters in Washington, D.C., guards the service's past and has been completely forthcoming with his archives. Indeed, all service personnel I contacted concerning this book took immediate and helpful interest in any way they could. Lt. Edwin H. Daniels Jr. is a perfect example. His love for *Eagle* and her traditions yielded not only an outpouring of advice and material but also much wit and wisdom, delivered with unique style and aplomb. Cmdr. James Loew, executive officer aboard *Eagle* during the 1985 season, tendered help without stint in the midst of enormous and far more serious responsibilities. Warrant Officer David Winchester, wry senior of *Eagle*'s engineering department, provided much perspective on the truth of ships. Rear Admiral Edward Nelson Jr., superintendent of the Coast Guard Academy, and Captain Joseph E. Vorbach, commandant of cadets at the Academy, not only blessed this project but also were the very best of shipmates—obviously proud of their ship and pleased with the charges in their responsibility.

Lt. (jg) Steven How, *Eagle*'s administrative officer, must receive special thanks. His ebullient passion for *Eagle* and its traditions and his ever-ready willingness to research the ship's history and personnel were inspiring. Too, Captain James G. Heydenreich (retired), former executive officer of *Eagle*, and Captain James P. Kelly (retired), former commanding officer and currently editor of the Academy's alumni bulletin, must receive special thanks. Their experience gave them canny judgment in addition to generous provision of photographic materials. Many thanks are also due Mr. Tido Holtkamp, whose reminiscences and personal cadet logs of the vessel's years under the German flag put flesh and blood on the skeletal legends of her early days.

On the personal front, dealing with a writer-friend under pressure can be at the least tedious and is seldom gratifying; and so my friends Peter Ralston, Marcus Halevi, and Philip Conkling herewith get nudges of appreciation, as do my wife, Victoria Dyer, and my children, Erik and Jessica Putz, each of whom added love and care, the absence of which I dare not consider.

The men and women of The Globe Pequot Press are a patient and professional team. Linda Kennedy, vice president–publications director and host of this project, was forthcoming and supportive from the beginning. Eric Newman's blue pencil is incisive yet kind—the best. Kate Bandos's care over the dissemination of information is like nothing seen heretofore in this life. Kevin Lynch's gifts turned words and images into beauty. Good books from nice, hard-working people.

To Llewellyn Howland III, my agent in these and other matters, thank you! This gentleman and scholar is a man of books, chief among them marine books, and is always of his word. Let's do, sir, go sailing.

Finally, any errors of fact or judgment in these pages are mine alone. The quality of help and friendship from all concerned is too high for it to be otherwise.

Foreword

by Walter Cronkite

There is a trouble with naval history. It has no seamarks.

There are landmarks in profusion to remind us of the rest of human experience. Crowds of visitors can visit in awe and wonder and respectful silence (or boisterous holiday hilarity) those sites where our laws were made, our philosophies honed, or our battles won. They can tread the very stone the ancients walked or gawk at the bed where the hero slept and the desk where he wrote. And they can read from bronze plaques and chiseled marble of the momentous events that occurred on the very spot. Landmarks of our past.

But there are no seamarks. There are tablets and monuments, of course, where persons or groups embarked or disembarked. On the dock at Falmouth, England, for instance, you can read that the Pilgrims departed from there, and at Provincetown and Plymouth, Massachusetts, you can read that they landed there. And in Boston you can see the house where Donald McKay lived when he designed the clipper ships.

But there are no seamarks. You can't walk the battlefields where Yankees and their ships proved with shot and shell that a young nation could defend its dream of independence and win its right to share equally the freedom of ocean trade. There are no trails by which to follow the paths of the merchant ships and whalers that carried the American flag to the earth's distant corners.

No, there are no seamarks. We have some very fine maritime museums where artifacts, and even ships, of our maritime heritage are lovingly preserved. That venerable battlelady *Constitution*, "Old Ironsides," launched in the first years of our nation and hero of the War of 1812, is a wonderful sight at her berth at the Charlestown Navy Yard, and an even more wonderful sight when, with flags flying and bands playing, she makes her annual excursion, under tow, out into Boston Harbor.

No, we have no seamarks — but we have something better. We have *Eagle*.

Here, in our country's only square-rigger still sailing, is a living reminder of our seagoing past, a monument that breathes, a vibrant, spirited descendant of every ship that ever flew the Stars and Stripes, her crew of

Coast Guard cadets the eager inheritors of the sailing tradition that built a nation.

Those young officers, upon graduation, will go to their arduous, sometimes dangerous, duties in modern vessels that burn diesel oil and are guided by unseen signals from radio towers and satellite transmitters, but they will take with them skills of seamanship and a respect for the sea that only a sailing ship can impart.

There is no experience, except perhaps those of soaring and ballooning, that can match sailing for the exciting challenge of pitting one's knowledge and skill against the forces of nature.

To sail is to enjoy the ultimate escape from the mundane; the waves against the hull and the wind in the rigging raise their voices in a song of liberty.

And that is the song that *Eagle* sings. With all sails flying and the wind in her teeth, the spray framing her bow and her foaming wake following true astern, she *is* freedom, a glorious confirmation of our past, a resplendent symbol of our future.

Americans share no other possession quite like her.

We will never have the opportunity to summon our strength and our courage to climb into her rigging and, high above her decks, sway precariously on her footropes as we hand and reef her mighty canvas in fair weather and terribly foul, nor shall we have the privilege of standing in dress uniform, proud on her crosstrees, as *Eagle* parades in the world's harbors.

But through this book we can enjoy vicariously the pride of the men and women who sail upon her, and we can rejoice again in all for which she stands.

Eagle — a unique, magnificent, majestic manifestation of the American spirit.

1 The United States Coast Guard Barque *Eagle*

Eagle is a special ship. As the only *seagoing* square-rigged vessel owned and operated by the United States, she sails for all Americans, as a ship of peace and peaceful order for all free peoples, and all people who would be free. The United States Coast Guard Academy in New London, Connecticut, has had *Eagle* in its stewardship for forty years, as its officer-cadet training ship. The kind and quality of this service is unique in modern times, and our purpose in this book is to tell *Eagle*'s story, to describe the ship and life aboard her, and to explain her purpose and accomplishments.

Nineteen-eighty-six is *Eagle*'s fiftieth-anniversary year. A half-century old, she not only has amassed stories, she is also a *grande dame* on the high seas. Like her nautical cousin, the U.S. Navy frigate *Constitution,* she has seen war, and she has seen on her decks trials of young sailors learning the ways of the sea. Though younger than the redoubtable lady Old Ironsides, *Eagle* has remained in seagoing service throughout her career. To this day, indeed on this day, *Eagle,* heels in the wind on assignment as an official operating cutter of the United States Coast Guard. Built to train, she trains. Assigned to guard, she guards. She is our ship, and this is her book.

Those who know and have feelings for the sea understand instinctively why a square-rigged ship is indispensable and has a place not only in the inventory of our military marine but also as an offering to the youth of our nation. *Eagle* is more than a school-ship or a training vessel for future Coast Guard officers; in her own way, she is a symbol of our country's roots in the maritime past and the nation's spirit that has always sought out and nurtured freedom by access to, and control of, the seas that surround us. Sailing ships brought many of our forebears here and then helped to feed and protect us, to found our modern idea of commerce, and to give opportunity to any and all with the imagination and pluck to go to sea. As a crux of our national defense, ships plumb the depths of the world's oceans and circumscribe the envelope of the atmosphere with all that contemporary technology offers; the fundamentals of nautical leadership happen on ships, and nowhere better than on a sailing ship. Matters of wind are the very stuff of navigation and piloting. Sail may no longer supply our civilization, but sail-training will never be archaic.

Water and land meet, and where they meet we are compelled to gather. The shore is far enough for some, but for others the sea roads call. By the sea, we are next to a highway that leads everywhere, all around the world. Boatmen and yachtsmen reach out, some sampling the waters seriously, even spectacularly. They cross oceans, have adventures in remote places, and regularly race through seas notorious for their hazards and challenges. Yet, the serious business of being at sea remains something of a mystery. Fishermen come and go, in and out of the harbor. They do not speak much. The mighty bulk-carrying traffic is these days directed outside our ordinary recreational purview. Where is the romance?

The myth remains embodied in the large square-rigged sailing ships. As marine societies, harbor development, nautical museums, and boatbuilding schools, boating programs, and festivals of sail proliferate, *Eagle* continues to do what she has always done. She does not deny the romance; she just naturally expresses it. Captain Christian, Admiral Nelson, Captains Courageous, and Billy Budd are no strangers to her — those characters in life and literature have always brought the nautically inclined to her, naturally.

For forty years visitors have come to docks, in America and abroad, to be next to the ship, to walk her decks, to be in direct contact with this barque that still participates in and practices the traditions of the sea in ways that only a deep-water sailing vessel can. When they do, the distinction between adult and child, parent and offspring often fades, as people of all ages and backgrounds picture themselves sailing the seas aboard *Eagle*, gazing up into the cloud of canvas sails in the rigging and feeling the broad decks heave and scend over the ocean's vast surface. Even experienced boatmen know that this ship offers something special that only blue-water square-rig sailors know.

The appeal is a mystery, some of which this book is meant to dispel, and some to keep. The marvel and romance of sailing ships are legendary because they are infinite. *Eagle* has plain duty, and the details of her existence and history are a matter of record, which will be the larger stuff of this book. As for the romance — romance has always meant devotion to an idea, empathy with others, expectation of trials that are regarded as a test of character and devotion, and a transfixed compulsion to beauty. Even in her most mundane functions as a military training vessel, *Eagle* is in all respects as ready for romance as she is for sea.

If these pages glow with the romance of the ship, our primary duty is to tell some of her background and history in an *Eagle* tradition, in our nation's eldest marine military service, and in her own right. We will explore her construction, how she is organized, and the changes that time have brought to her layout, from stem to stern, keel to mastcap. A working ship, *Eagle* is generally a hive of nautical activity, and so we will in words and pictures go aboard the ship, sail her, live with the complement of men and women who command and sail her, and probe some of her human secrets and stories. Fifty years of continuous duty produces tales to tell and a society of the ship's own, now many service generations deep. And finally we will consider *Eagle's* role as a training vessel, schooling seamen in the highest order of nautical education, as an ambassador of the service and nation, and as a tall ship in an international community that at its best knows what sailors on the world's oceans have always known, that the best service works toward peace. *Eagle* has trained more than 5,000 United States Coast Guard officers since 1946, and, unique in America's fleet, she stands by to do so again.

Eagle's Background 2

While I recommend in the strongest terms to the respective Officers, activity, vigilance and firmness, I feel no less solicitude that their deportment may be marked with prudence, moderation and good temper. Upon these last qualities not less than upon the former must depend the success, usefulness, and consequently *continuance* of the establishment in which they are included. They cannot be sensible that there are some prepossessions against it, that the charge with which they are entrusted is a delicate one, and that it is easy by mismanagement to produce serious and extensive clamour, disgust and odium.

They will always keep in mind that their Countrymen are Freemen and as such are impatient of every thing that bears the least mark of domineering Spirit. They will therefore refrain with the most guarded circumspection from whatever has the semblance of haughtiness, rudeness or insult. If obstacles occur they will remember they are under the particular protection of the Laws, and that they can meet with nothing disagreeable in the execution of their duty which these will not severely reprehend. This reflection and a regard to the good of the service will prevent at all times a spirit of irritation or resentment. They will endeavour to overcome difficulties, if any are experienced, by a cool and temperate perseverance in their duty, by address and moderation rather than by vehemence or violence.

Thus, in a Treasury Department circular to the captains of the Revenue Cutters, Alexander Hamilton admonished his charges on June 4, 1791.

Just two years before, George Washington had assumed office as our first president, facing a new nation with no administrative branches of government. Both Britain and Spain still occupied ostensibly American lands, the remaining army was minuscule, and the navy had been disbanded. In the western territories already talk of secession spread. The government was in debt, both to its own citizens and to foreign persons and corporations — and the treasury, if such it could be called, was barren. Although Congress had passed an import tariff for revenue, it had no means for collecting revenue. Though jubilant and proud of defeating an empire, the citizenry had yet to fully realize the responsibilities of citizenship. A century of cynicism about authority and Caesar's rendering in a colonial atmosphere had made smuggling and duplicitous behavior a cherished habit. Americans were a maritime people, and able sailors. Dark of night and small creeks and coves held no fear and little danger for them, except that now they were cheating their own government, and so, by the Constitution, themselves.

Under Alexander Hamilton, the new Treasury Department's mandate (created September 2, 1789) was to improve and manage revenues for the support of public credit; to estimate public revenues and expenditures; and to otherwise manage the public lands and purse strings. From the beginning this responsibility included collecting customs duties, running the lighthouse service, and managing the bureaucratic machinery for the registration and clearance of seagoing vessels. By the time the Federalists left office in 1801, the Treasury Department had become the largest organ of the government, employing fully half the civilian public work force. Among these were the collectors of customs at the ports, and because their salaries came directly out of what they collected, their collective hue and cry over means for intercepting vessels at sea, before they had a chance to discharge cargoes or alter their bills of lading, demanded that something be done, and quickly.

On April 23, 1790, therefore, Hamilton presented to Congress a bill to establish the United States Revenue Marine Service. "Boats," he declared, could not "fail to contribute, in a material degree, to the security of the revenue; much more than will compensate for the expense of the establishment...." He went on:

> Justice to the body of Merchants of the United States, demands an acknowledgement, that they have very generally manifested a disposition to conform to the national laws, which does them honor, and authorizes confidence in their probity. But every considerate member of that body knows that this confidence admits of exceptions, and that it is essentially the interest of the greater number, that every possible guard should be set on the fraudulent few, which does not in fact tend to the embarrassment of trade.

He proposed that ten revenue cutters be constructed, to be stationed along the coasts of Massachusetts and New Hampshire (two), Long Island Sound (one), New York and Delaware Bay (one each), the Chesapeake (two), and one each for North Carolina, South Carolina, and Georgia. The young secretary estimated that each vessel would cost $1,000 to construct, and that an annual budget of $18,560 would be adequate to maintain all expenses of the entire fleet. Congress passed the bill on August 4, 1790, giving birth to the parent organization of the United States Coast Guard. One of the first vessels built for the new Revenue Cutter Service was a vessel named *Eagle*.

The clouds of time have obscured this schooner from our view. We know that she displaced about 50 tons, was 50 feet long on the deck, and carried topsails on both her fore and main topmasts. She was ordered built along with her sister vessels in 1791, at Savannah, Georgia, under the supervision of John Howell, who was commissioned as her master when the vessel

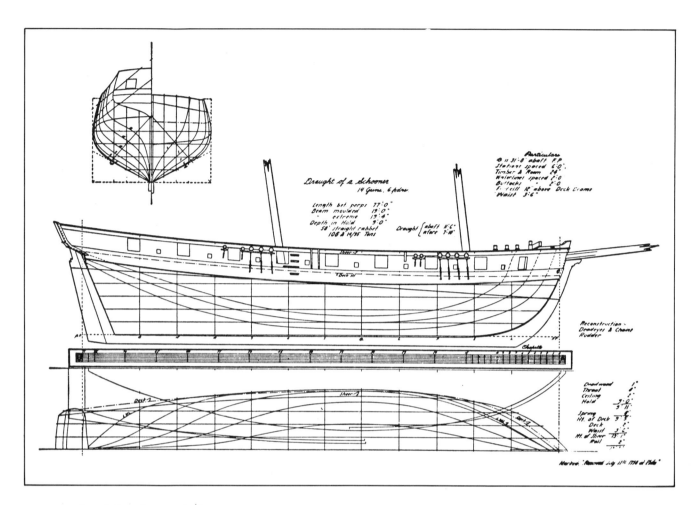

was completed, less her sails, by December in the following year. Though a few of the standard secondary sources refer to this ship as the *Pickering,* primary newspaper sources of the day call her *Eagle,* and so she becomes here the first of our *Eagle*s, of which seven in all were built, including our present steel barque, in the service of the Coast Guard and its paternal organizations.

As nearly as we can tell, the first *Eagle* remained in service at least until 1798. Historical and social changes were coming thick and fast as the eighteenth century drew to a close, and the clarity of events and their attendant names are sometimes not what they should be; an example being conditions surrounding the first *Eagle's* replacement. For, you see, in 1799, *Eagle* was replaced by a ship named *Bee,* a renamed captured French vessel, *Bon Père* (Good Father), which in spring 1799 had been captured by a revenue cutter named *Eagle* — not the first *Eagle,* but rather a second one.

This vagueness is one of those things that give historians their employment. Just as the naval-history sources are confused over the dates, places, and names germane to the first *Eagle,* the second *Eagle,* too, suffers from fuzzy documentation and reportage. The most likely marshaling of facts is that the first *Eagle,* operating out of Georgia, was sold out of service in

The lines and plans of America's first ten revenue cutters are lost. But in The History of the American Sailing Navy *(Norton, 1949), Howard I. Chapelle shows this unidentified fourteen-gun schooner of the same period. It must be similar to the first* Eagle, *though the latter was a bit smaller and probably had no gunports.*

early 1798, and replaced by a brig renamed *Eagle* in late 1798; a likely theory, for all but one of the first ten revenue cutters had been replaced by 1800. Readers who enjoy untangling such puzzles of nautical history will find a good place to start in Irving H. King's *George Washington's Coast Guard* (Annapolis: Naval Institute, 1978); Paul Johnson's excellent first chapter in Paul Regan's *Eagle Seamanship* (Annapolis: Naval Institute, 1979); and two of Howard Chapelle's classics: *The History of the American Sailing Navy* and *The History of American Sailing Ships* (both New York: W. W. Norton).

Our second *Eagle,* a brig, had a neat and compact square-rigged arrangement that, along with the schooner rig, Americans brought to great efficiency in early days. This setup has an exclusively square-rigged foremast and a combination square and fore-and-aft rigged mizzen, or aftermast. Built in Philadelphia in 1798, *Eagle II* was 58 feet overall, and displaced 187 tons, very substantial for her length. Carrying a crew of seventy men, including fourteen marines, and ordnance composed of fourteen six-pounder cannon, she had to be solid, and she certainly distinguished herself.

These were the days of the Quasi-War with France, the official designation for one of our most peculiar conflicts as a nation. With three- or four-score vessels always operating in the Caribbean at any one time, the new French republic was wont to do as it pleased, and if this liberty led to taking American ships as "prizes," it felt no qualms. Accordingly, four relatively large squadrons of U.S. ships were dispatched to deal with the Frankish menace, most of it by letters of marque, a tactic familiar from the revolutionary period, and much of it oddly nonviolent, extending only to intimidation such as warning shots. French ships would bring our ships to stays, stopping them, and board them with prize crews; then our ships would recapture our vessels, or similarly capture originally French vessels. Mr. Johnson renders this report in *Eagle Seamanship:*

> In the West Indies from 1798 to 1800, the *Eagle* was one of the most successful ships, first in the squadron of Stephen Decatur, Sr., later in that of Commodore John Barry. In all, *Eagle* captured five French armed vessels. On two other occasions, she assisted the ships *Delaware* and *Baltimore* in taking prizes. In addition, several American merchant vessels captured by the French were retaken by the *Eagle*. One of her best captures was the schooner *Bon Père,* which was renamed *Bee* and used by American forces.

Eagle was sold into private hands, in 1801, for $10,600.

In the meanwhile, the revenue-cutter service, having firmly established reliable collection of duties, and having enfranchised itself as integral to naval defense, had taken on full responsibility for putting out and maintaining aids to navigation, assisting the keepers of the nation's lighthouses, beginning the intricate task of charting our coasts, and habitually coming to the aid of distressed vessels and mariners. By the time the second *Eagle* was mustered out of service, nearly all duties handled by the modern Coast Guard were operational.

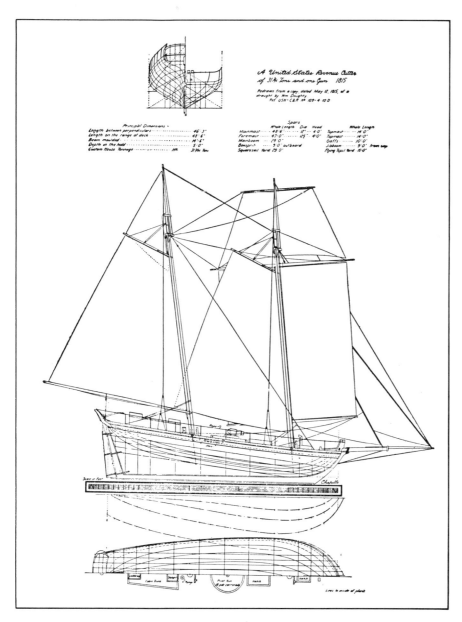

Though able and hardworking, the first ten little revenue cutters were soon too small, slow, and few for the nation's growing economic needs and were overshadowed by the explosion in shipping following the French Revolution. By 1800, all but one of the original cutters had been replaced by larger ships. The second and third Eagles were, respectively, a brig of a type shown here in two sizes, and a topsail schooner shown here in quarter-elevated view and at sea. (These and the illustrations on page 13 are from Howard I. Chapelle, *American Sailing Ships* [Norton, 1935].)

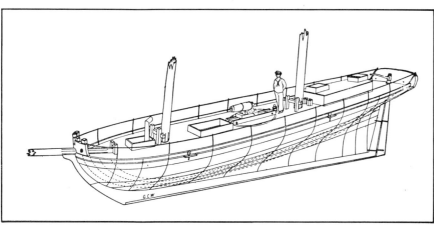

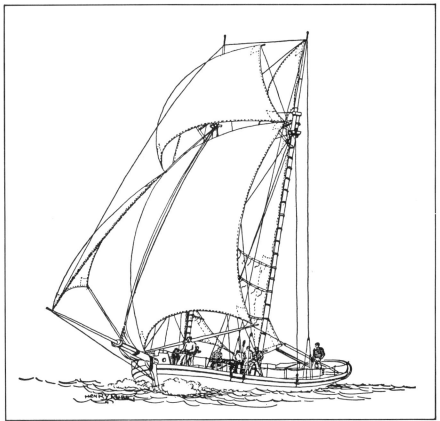

Deep-water altercations with French ships had occasionally harassed our commerce, but more and more our vigorous merchants had to deal with English bottoms. Those of imperial sentiments were naturally contemptuous of postcolonial upstarts, and American English had not yet shifted enough from English speech to provide the ostensible badge of independent citizenship. President James Madison declared war in 1812 over impressment of American sailors and other harassments by the English, who, until 1814, were distracted by Napoleon's navy. Once Elba became the able Corsican's home in exile, however, the British threw their full naval weight against the North American coastline, and from that period come many stories about our most famous naval acts of heroism, among them that of the third U.S. ship called *Eagle*.

The new *Eagle* was again a schooner, of 130 tons, built in and for the port of New Haven in 1809. She was lightly armed (four four-pound, and two two-pound cannons), and her ordinary duty was to patrol and escort merchant shipping to and from the Connecticut shore and New York. Once the English bottoms were up to strength in the region, in 1814, her duty led to heroism, then demise.

The sloop *Susan* was a regular New Haven–New York packet, and in

Eagle II (left), a very active armed brig with a full complement of marines, engages the French in the Quasi-War with France in 1799. (Artist unknown; reproduction courtesy of U.S.C.G. Academy Museum, Paul Johnson, curator)

After a running battle with the English in 1814, Eagle *III's officers and crew beach the ship and heroically stand off the enemy at Negro Head on the Connecticut shore. Eventually reduced to using the ship's log as wadding to pack the ordnance charges, they won the battle if not the campaign. Next day,* Eagle *was captured and, soon after, scuttled. (Painting by Hunter Wood; reproduction courtesy U.S. Coast Guard Academy Museum, Paul Johnson, curator)*

autumn 1814, laden with flour, gunpowder, dry goods, and passengers, she was intercepted and captured by the English frigate *Pomone.* Incensed and determined to bring the home sloop back, Captain Frederick Lee of *Eagle* recruited thirty extra men to man the ship and made out to sea, not knowing the mischief that lay in wait: the eighteen-gun British brig *Dispatch,* accompanied by her armed tender and another armed sloop. Bravado and ire notwithstanding, *Eagle* made for the Long Island shore. There, at Negro Head, *Eagle's* company managed to drag four of the ship's guns to the bluff above the ship, and from there they fended off the attacking vessels for many hours, and through the night. In the interim, the Americans were reduced to using their clothing, and even sheets torn from the ship's log, for cannon wadding, to back recycled shot provided by the English onslaught. By morning the enemy had withdrawn, leaving *Eagle* a hulk. Though the crew at length refloated the ship, her bedraggled condition invited capture on the return passage across the Sound. Captured she was, and retired from history. Presumably, she was stripped and scuttled.

The same fate fell upon many American vessels, which, even when spared battle fatigue, were becoming elderly by 1814. Though all of coastal America was a riot of boat- and shipbuilding, most marine activity was in the name of commerce, and the government's efforts to lead in the field had been applied to line fleet vessels, notorious then as now for absorbing all allocated monies. With treaties signed and a maritime populace growing in number and activity annually (the interior was opening up and industry becoming well established), revenue and navigation-maintenance vessels were needed more than ever. They also had to be faster.

The chase had become a mutually escalating race between those bound to catch, and those who would not be caught. Sailing technology reached its best off the coast of Africa, where the British blockade against slavers called for fine-lined, shallow-draft, wide hulls carrying clouds of sail. Handy and quick, these new Baltimore clippers could sail into the shallows of inshore creeks and bays, and yet run transatlantic circles around the ponderous, bluff-bowed gunnery platforms that warships had to be. As the bad guys refined their sailing hardware, so the Revenue Service had to keep up, with three new classes of cutters, all of the Baltimore clipper type. Two of these carried the name *Eagle* in the years from 1815 through the early 1830s.

William Doughty, a well-known designer in that era, had the commission for all three standard classes, respectively 49, 57, and 69 feet overall, all with more or less the same hull model and proportions. Both *Eagles IV* and *V* were of the 69-foot class, displacing 79 tons. Except for the continuity of fate reigning over these ships, we know rather little about them. One was built at New York and served out of New Haven from 1816 to 1824; the next was built in 1824 at Portsmouth, New Hampshire, and also served New Haven until 1829. Both of these were commanded throughout their duty by Frederick Lee, who had shepherded *Eagle III* through its demise in the war. By the Jacksonian period, *Eagle*s and the Connecticut shore were lastingly associated.

This historical line was broken for almost a century. Then in fall 1925, a 100-foot motor patrol boat, one of thirteen in a class-building program, was launched as *Eagle,* from the Defoe facilities in Bay City, Michigan. Her duty was patroling for rumrunners during Prohibition out of New London, Connecticut, for seven years, and from Charleston, South Carolina, until that sad social program was ended. The sixth *Eagle*'s duty was enlivened by the craziness inherent in the liquor-smuggling trade, as when the booze supply ship *Firelight* attempted to ram *Eagle* and instead sprang her own planks and sank. Adequately armed but relatively slow, *Eagle* ended her career by serving a year at the Charlotte, New York, station on Lake Ontario. *Our Eagle,* the seventh, would not serve us until a Great Depression and a horrendous war had gone by.

The Service and Its Academy

The United States Coast Guard celebrates several banner dates among its traditions. The first is August 4, 1790, when Congress officially created the Revenue Marine; on June 18, 1878, Congress created the U.S. Life Saving Service; on June 18, 1915, the Revenue Cutter Service was combined with the Life Saving Service to compose the United States Coast Guard; and on July 7, 1939, the Lighthouse Bureau was absorbed by the Coast Guard. On a less-celebrated day in May 1877, aboard topsail schooner *J. C. Dobbin,* Captain J. A. Henriques employed his commissioned and enlisted officers to create a curriculum in seamanship and navigation, which was promptly used in training young cadet officers in the waters between the eastern

By the Jacksonian era the revenue cutters had a basic form and design. It was based on the very fast Baltimore-clipper models popular among the slavers and smugglers with which the Revenue Marine had to contend. The fifth and sixth Eagles *were of this type, shown here in fore-quarter elevated view and at sea. The drawings are based on a near-sister cutter of the period. By this time a fundamental family resemblance to our (seventh)* Eagle *is visible.*

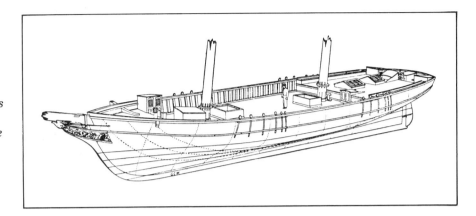

seaboard and Bermuda. In autumn that year, the *Dobbin* put into New Bedford, Massachusetts, and her wardroom officers added academic subjects to the new program, hiring a civilian professor to teach them. The founding concepts and practices of the U.S. Coast Guard Academy were thus established.

The 106-foot barque *Chase* replaced the *J. C. Dobbin* in the next year, and this ship, the namesake for vessels fondly held in Coast Guard memory, was the Academy training home until 1894, out of New Bedford, and until 1907, at winter quarters on Arundel Cove, in Maryland. *Chase* began the Coast Guard Academy tradition of cadet summer cruises to Europe and continued reliably for two decades.

Before the era of *Eagles*, half a dozen other training ships entered the Academy fleet. From 1907 until 1921 the choice was *Itasca*, formerly Navy practice ship *Bancroft*, and then *Alexander Hamilton*, the former Navy gunboat *Vicksburg* and a veteran of the China station. In the meanwhile, the official Coast Guard Academy was moved from Arundel Cove to New

London, at first ensconced in Fort Trumbull (from 1910) and finally to its present site on the banks of the Thames River in 1932.

The *Alexander Hamilton* was retired in 1930, and from then until *Eagle* arrived in 1946, the Academy's fleet was catch-as-catch-can, but still distinguished. The veteran Gloucester fishing schooner *J. C. Dobbin II,* renamed *Chase,* served its time in the 1930s, as did the well-known yacht *Curlew* and the fabulous three-masted schooner *Atlantic.* Present-day yachtsmen and women would give their eyeteeth to experience such ships under canvas.

World War II was devastating to all discretionary boats and boating. As of November 1, 1941, the Coast Guard was placed under the Navy Department, whose priorities naturally brought all available bottoms into active service, or out of commission to languish ashore, or sequestered for precious lead and nonferrous scrap. Sail training did not loom large on the defense horizon. On the fateful day when Hitler's troops marched into Denmark, however, the Danish training vessel *Danmark* was on a training cruise, visiting Jacksonville, Florida. Captain Kurt L. Hansen of the *Danmark* found himself in a welter of Southern hospitality as local citizens provided food, clothing, and entertainment for the young Danish sailors.

Knud Langvad (third left), alumnus of Eagle *from her delivery voyage to the United States in 1946, talks over the old days with Rear Admiral Edward Nelson Jr. (center), superintendent of the Coast Guard Academy; Captain Ernst Cummings (far right), commanding officer of* Eagle; *and guests in the ship's wardroom during a spring 1985 visit.* (U.S. Coast Guard photo by Indie Williams)

In the presence of Adolf Hitler and the German Navy high command, Horst Wessel *is launched in 1936 at the famed shipyard of Blohm & Voss in Hamburg.* (U.S. Coast Guard photo, originally published in *Der Stern;* donated by Klaus Willeke)

Hearing of *Danmark*'s situation, the commandant of the Coast Guard approached the Danish legation (in exile) and offered to charter the vessel for training service at the Coast Guard Academy. This request was granted, and so from Janury 1942 until September 1945, Denmark's first-class ship sailed the relatively protected inshore waters of Long Island Sound and around the Massachusetts islands, off Cape Cod. Along with *Eagle, Danmark* remains one of the most popular and best-run tall ships in the world, and her inadvertent tour of wartime duty with the United States is commemorated on a plaque displayed on the Dane's mainmast. Captain Knud Langvad had accompanied *Eagle* on its delivery to the United States in 1946, and it was a fine reunion when, in spring 1985, Captain Langvad, age seventy-seven, was ship's guest aboard *Eagle* for the first time in thirty-nine years.

Our Barque *Eagle*

Billeted aboard *Danmark* during her tour under U.S. colors was Commander Gordon P. McGowan, who was assigned aboard as director of the Academy's sailing and seamanship-training program. In his fascinating *The Skipper and the Eagle,* McGowan admits to being nearly a passenger aboard *Danmark,* for the ability and verve of the officers and seamen native to the vessel embarrassed any inclination to intervene or assume authority. The commander himself became a cadet of sorts, watching the ways of the 700-ton square-rigger without the slightest suspicion of the consequences these wartime days would have. These were introduced to him by telegram late in autumn 1945. *Danmark* had been repatriated a couple of months before, placing the thirty-six-year-old commander on the beach. His telegram read:

> ON OR ABOUT 18 JANUARY 1946 PROCEED BY AIR TO LONDON
> ENGLAND AND REPORT TO COMNAVEU FOR FURTHER
> ASSIGNMENT AS PROSPECTIVE COMMANDING OFFICER OF
> THE COAST GUARD CUTTER EAGLE NOW THE GERMAN
> EX-NAVAL SHIP HORST WESSEL AT THE U S NAVAL ADVANCE
> BASE WESER RIVER BREMERHAVEN GERMANY.

Horst Wessel, soon to become *Eagle,* lay at a wharfside tidal berth, and though she was still manned by a marginally employed German navy crew, her condition was shabby, exhausted by the war. Much of Bremerhaven was dusty piles of rubble.

Sail-training vessels had been in the German naval tradition since the nineteenth century, and these were revitalized under the vigorous rearmament programs of the Third Reich. Between 1933 and 1940, the Germans built five training barques: in 1933 *Gorch Fock,* in 1936 *Horst Wessel* (our *Eagle*), in 1938 *Albert Leo Schlageter* and *Mircea II,* and in 1940 *Herbert Norkus.* All five vessels were built on nearly identical lines and layouts, differing only a few feet in length, and in minor details of rigging and deck

Horst Wessel, *years later to become* Eagle, *sails her builder's trials for Blohm & Voss off the River Elbe estuary, 1936.* (U.S. Coast Guard Academy Museum Archives photo)

Three of the original Five Sisters line up at wharfside in their early days: Gorch Fock, Horst Wessel, *and* Albert Leo Schlageter, *now, respectively,* Tovarishch, Eagle *and* Sagres II. *History has turned matters on their head but has left undiminished the beauty and service of these extraordinary ships.* (U.S. Coast Guard Academy Museum Archives photo, German origin unknown)

Kapitan August Thiele, for three years (1936–39) the first commanding officer of Horst Wessel. *His first season or two took the ship into the North Atlantic as far as the West Indies. Thereafter it was confined to the eastern Baltic.* (U.S Coast Guard photo, donated by Klaus Willeke)

layout. The other sister ships may interest tall-ship enthusiasts. At war's end, *Gorch Fock* disappeared into Soviet mists, returning to public view in the mid-1950s as *Tovarishch*. *Horst Wessel* became our *Eagle*. *Albert Leo Schlageter* lay in a mud berth near *Eagle* on the day the latter sailed away from Germany, eventually to be claimed by Brazil. There she sailed first as *Guna Bara,* and today as *Sagres II,* under Portuguese colors. *Mircea* came to serve under the Romanian flag. *Herbert Norkus,* built during the war, was never rigged; she served as an ammunition storage depot for the Germans. After the war, the British used the still-new hull as a North Sea disposal barge, opening the sea cocks to sink her on the final tow voyage. To this day, many English sailors lament that event. All five ships were built at the famed Blohm & Voss shipyard in Hamburg, to very high standards of strength, sailing ability, and safety. The German High Command had plans for these vessels' charges; eventually, they were used mostly to train navy personnel as submarine officers, scourges of the North Atlantic shipping lanes. The ships embodied the very best that naval architecture and construction systems of the time had to offer, superb even by today's standards.

These days, the original sister ships *Tovarishch* (the *original Gorch*

Fock), Eagle, Sagres II, and *Mircea* still sail together in the major tall-ships events, joined for the Five Sisters' Cup by *Gorch Fock II* (a replica sister vessel built by West Germany in 1958) in occasional extraordinary races.

In 1986, *Eagle* (ex–*Horst Wessel*) is fifty years old and from a time and place that seems like an altogether different world, uncanny even for those with memories of Europe during the Depression years. In its own way, that era was also a period of extraordinary technological advances, much like those of today, but in mechanics rather than the hyperelectronics in which we bask. Shipbuilding was one of these fields, and German shipyards were on the cutting edge. Only a generation before, builders of iron and steel ships were still bogged down in design and engineering practices essentially derived from wood shipbuilding technologies — massive timbering. As metallurgy, forging, and plate-bending methods improved, though, and engineers gained experience with massive metal construction, especially in steel, mathematical formulas for stress, load, and tension replaced bulky materials. Even as ships became lighter they became stronger, and with improved power plants, much faster and generally more able.

And so the transverse framing system was developed. This construction method employs the inherent strength of steel, wherever it is in the ship, to provide integrity, rather than large amounts of support behind or around it. *Eagle's* keel, main deck, and hull plating provide the primary strength of the vessel, and her light framing, incorrectly called ribs, is used primarily to hold the vessel's shape. Modern engineering and welding methods have superseded the basic technology applied in *Eagle*. These German-built training barques especially benefited from the savings in weight provided by this building method. In a sailing ship with youngsters aboard, the more

Kadett Tido Holtkamp, 1944. (Courtesy Tido Holtkamp)

German Navy crewmen from Horst Wessel *conduct boat drills off the dramatic Tenerife coast in 1938, a year before the invasion of Poland and World War II.* (U.S. Coast Guard photo, donated by Klaus Willeke)

Tido Holtkamp today. (Courtesy Tido Holtkamp)

weight placed in ballast, far down in the bilges, the better, for the ships must be able to stand up to indiscretion, error, and flawed nautical judgment.

Horst Wessel went right into service after being fitted out, sailing her first full season (1937) in the open Atlantic and paying calls in the Canary Islands and the West Indies. After hostilities began, with Hitler's invasion of Poland in 1939, the ship was confined to duty in the Baltic, more or less out of harm's way for her cadets, as they made training and, later, refugee and supply runs between ports such as Danzig (now Gdansk) and East Prussia. Stories told among alumni of the ship, that she was fired upon at least once and returned fire against Allied planes, have not been verified. Indeed, the only encounters under arms that we could discover were related by Tido Holtkamp, a German cadet on the ship during spring 1944 — close calls in night bombing raids and one misunderstanding with a German reconnaissance plane. Today an American citizen and a senior industrial applications consultant for IBM, Holtkamp recalls his own experiences on the ship. He assiduously followed the course of battles near and far, imagining what it was like at the fronts, meanwhile coursing through Baltic waters. The ship had two genuine adventures during his tenure: hove to outside Kiel Harbor while both town and harbor structures were destroyed by bombs; and shooting at a seaplane that was reconnoitering the ship. Warned in code several times, the pilot failed to respond

Exercises in the Baltic in 1938 brought Horst Wessel *close to shore at sea-furl and dress whites in the rigging. Such drills are universal on square-riggers, at all times, among all nations. It is part of ship's routine, cherished by enthusiasts of blue-water sailing.* (U.S. Coast Guard Academy Museum Archives photo)

Horst Wessel crew members singing sea-chanteys as they bring up the anchor chain in the Baltic Sea off Danzig (now Gdansk), spring 1944. Two-and-a-half rotations of the capstan were required to raise the chain one meter; at times it was as deep as 270 meters. Note 20 mm gun at right. (Courtesy Tido Holtkamp)

correctly. Manning three of the vessel's four 20 mm pom-pom guns, Holtkamp and his shipmates fired on the plane. At this act, the pilot cranked his aircraft into a full banked turn, revealing the iron crosses emblazoned on the wings, and then set it down on the water. Soon an inflatable boat that appeared near the plane's pontoons brought a thoroughly enraged pilot alongside the ship, demanding to see the skipper and his logbooks. Sure enough, the ship was twenty-four hours behind in its code manifest, which changed every twelve hours. It was not an especially good day for *Horst Wessel.* Crack gunners aboard could have made it even poorer.

Morning wash with salt water on Horst Wessel *deck, 1944. Cadets were required to wash in this manner from February 1 on, then run through a hose's powerful stream, all in order to "toughen" them and ensure that they were free from colds, according to former cadet Tido Holtkamp, shown at right. There were regular washrooms below deck, and freshwater showers were available in the evening.* (Courtesy Tido Holtkamp)

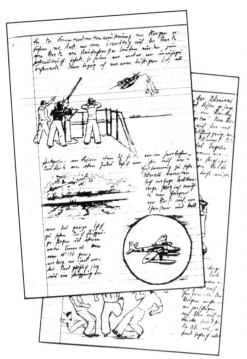

A page from Tido Holtkamp's logbook describing the misadventure with a seaplane described in the text. All the German cadets were required to keep such a record of their shipboard experiences, to be reviewed periodically by the division officer. This one survives because Mr. Holtkamp had the foresight to mail it home before the Germans surrendered. (Courtesy Tido Holtkamp)

In the class after Mr. Holtkamp's, the last, word spread among the cadets that they were destined for the new class-23 submarines, ten of which had already been launched with considerable effect. But, as German efforts on all sides decayed into a rout, the ship turned to transporting refugees from East Prussia. On the day of capitulation, the ship lay at Flensburg. Paging through the logbook he had kept while a cadet, the gracefully aging Teuton reflected on it all. Those verses of the German national anthem, nearly always followed by the insipid four verses of the "Horst Wessel" song, with arm outstretched in the Nazi salute, had seemed interminable. And when security demands removed the vessel's name from the sailors' cap ribbons, many of the crew were relieved. No love was lost between the German navy and its National Socialist overseers, but even at that, the namesake, a particularly pugnacious lieutenant of Hitler's early days, galled even the most loyal cadets. Of course, events soon changed everything.

When it became clear to Grand Admiral Doenitz that articles of surrender were imminent, the admiral, anticipating terrible repercussions that could issue from Hitler's tattered headquarters, gave out general orders to the entire German navy to "capitulate in a legal and orderly fashion." This directive contravened a standing order from the High Command that all navy vessels were to be scuttled, destroyed in the face of possible capture. Months after the war had ended, the German skipper of *Horst Wessel* personally conducted Commander McGowan to the place in the ship where permanent blasting charges had been installed, explaining how he had gathered about himself the most emotionally stable men in the ship to stand guard while he dismantled the firing mechanism. This step accomplished, the future *Eagle* needed only time and care to enter a happier career.

Germany was in ruins, and occupying forces had commandeered much of whatever habitable and operable facilities remained. All German military

German naval cadets in the old berthing area, a scene common below-decks well into our own era, when hammocks were the sleeping bill of fare until they were replaced by bunks installed in many subdivided areas of the ship. (U.S. Coast Guard Academy photo, courtesy James Heydenreich)

personnel were placed under the various Allied military commands, which for the most part held everyone where they were at the time of surrender, until work assignments could be found for them. The sailors aboard *Horst Wessel* generally had no idea whether they yet had homes to which to return, and at first no way to get to them if they did. They stayed aboard the ship. Meanwhile, Allied Headquarters had sequestered all German ships, and published a list of them as a reparations manifest. A large book could be written about how the Allies untangled the reparations problem, but on the surface, at least, much of the activity seems to have been done with mirrors, through a vast network of informal deals and agreements made by people whose only authority to do so was gumption, if not gall. Things were too chaotic for it to be otherwise. Commander McGowan's chronicle of how *Horst Wessel* was converted to *Eagle* is full of extraordinary happenstance, personal dealings, and luck, beginning when the superintendent of the Coast Guard Academy heard of the sailing barque's availability in Germany and promptly moved to get hold of it. Dispatching McGowan and ten other commissioned officers and enlisted personnel to take it all in hand, in a national context of nearly frantic disarmament, was an act of great imagination.

With some levity, McGowan recounts the frustration of trying to get things done in a world enervated by war. His transatlantic flight from New York to London — via Labrador, Iceland, and Scotland, in a reluctant C-54 — took six days, hinting at the difficulties to come. When finally he located the ship:

> She lay at a bombed-out shipyard amid the ugly skeletons of shattered buildings and mountainous heaps of rubble, her stately masts canted drunkenly to starboard, as she rested on the bottom of a narrow waterway at low tide. Her gray sides were smeared with stains, the paint on her yards and masts blistered and cracked. Raised metal lettering on each side of the quarterdeck informed the world that this was *Horst Wessel,* a ship of the dead Nazi navy.

McGowan's orders were to fit out the ship, making her ready for sea in all respects, and then to sail the ship, at his discretion, by any route, on any schedule possible, back to America. *In* doing this job, he was not to cost the United States any monies whatever — not one dime. *To* do so, he had only a decommissioned ship, a few colleagues, and a skeleton, half-starved German crew; and no tools, no rigging rope, no sails, no ship's stores, no engine, no paint or maintenance materials, no electrical supplies, and no prospect of a sailing crew adequate to get a 300-foot square-rigger across the ocean. Five months later *Eagle* was a fully found, fully commissioned cutter of the United States Coast Guard, on her way to her new home at New London. Every last acquisition and task required by the project was found, cajoled, badgered, wheeled-and-dealed in the midst of the mayhem that was northern Germany. A few highlights from a great many:

The Engine. The early weeks of the project were naturally given over to diagnosis, so that an orderly needs assessment could be prepared, if not

A blasted-out window frames Horst Wessel *during her fitting out to become* Eagle, *amid the ruins of Bremerhaven and its Weser River harbor, during the hard and unsure spring of 1946.* (U.S. Coast Guard Archives photo)

necessarily a proper work schedule. At first no one knew where anything was or might be sought, but a comprehensive list of needs would at least give everyone the wavelengths to which to tune their scrounging antennas.

The ship's small engine room was dominated by a large, slow-turning M.A.N. (Maschinenfabrik Augsburg-Nurnberg, the firm that built it) diesel, used primarily for calm weather, negotiating harbors, and docking maneuvers. When McGowan's engineering officer dismantled this behemoth (based on a 1932 design), it was found to be shot through with microcracks, indicating mere hours of running time left in its tired corpus. The nameplate on the engine gave an Augsburg address, to which the supply officer was dispatched, posthaste; there he discovered that the plant had been turned over to the British, who used its facilities to supply the huge minesweeping effort going on in the North Sea. British Navy headquarters was in Hamburg, where the good commander went for an interview with the good commodore:

> Upon entering his office, I noted a distinct chill in the air. The Commodore appeared to be well past sixty. Barely acknowledging our introduction, he peered at me through frigid blue eyes. A pair of horn-rimmed glasses skidded down toward the tip of his nose. He took

my measure while I squirmed inwardly. The cool reception and the level, wordless stare had the desired effect of intimidation. I had the feeling that anything I might say would certainly sound idiotic. I went completely on the defensive as he casually picked me to pieces with questions. It was obvious that the Yanks weren't going to get a damn thing at the expense of the precious mine-sweeping program. I felt that I had my answer wrapped up in a neat package before I had even made my request. When I finally blurted out my proposition, a new engine block from his factory, he fell silent. I supposed he was composing some Noel Cowardish answer.

The Commodore's gaze fastened upon the gold shield on my sleeve. His expression changed.

"I say, Coast Guard, are you?"

I admitted it.

Whereupon, he called in a stenographer and dictated a letter authorizing free access to the Augsburg factory, and gave me assurance that we could have "any bleeding thing" we wanted.

"The Coast Guard's no stranger to me, y'know. I rode one of your stout little craft here and there in the channel on 'D' day. Picked up dozens of flyers swimming about. Coast Guard chap got decorated. Damn fine show. Met other Coast Guard vessels before and after 'D' day. They were smart vessels. Glad to help with the *Horst Wessel* if she's for your branch.

"My dear chap, you must let us give you lunch. Terribly sorry I cawn't be there. Must dash off to Cuxhaven. I'm the great loser, y'know. Would love to sit and talk Coast Guard."

Rope and Tools. The ship's supply lockers were destitute. The German skipper said that once the air raids had begun, all supplies had been cut off, and the best hope was that underground stashes might be found. And so it

Coast Guardsmen wrestle with bits of pieces of the ship's M.A.N. diesel engine under arduous post-war conditions. A stroke of good fortune and English good will provided a usable replacement block, but the entire engine remained in use until its replacement in 1982. (U.S. Coast Guard Archives photo)

was for many of this ship's needs, but her rope and marlinspike supplies came by an almost surreally standard source, amid the conditions that prevailed in the former war zone. Columbus Key, on Germany's North Coast, had been allotted to the American occupying forces, so that they could have access to a major port in relatively good condition. Formerly a cruise-liner embarkation port, and not heavily bombed, rumors that a large, sealed, navy-held warehouse there might contain ship's stores were more than a little intriguing.

With all the windows shuttered, the interior of the lower floor was almost completely dark. I stood a while, waiting for my eyes to adjust to the gloom. Yanking out a handkerchief, I polished my glasses. Faintly at first, bulky objects began to appear. Row upon row of coils of rope materialized. I approached a coil and picked up a loose end protruding from the top. Here before me lay a five-foot thick coil of new five-inch Manila line, the exact thing so badly needed to replace the tattered tacks and sheets of the lower courses of the *Horst Wessel*. A surge of excitement mushroomed inside me. There beyond lay another coil and another! They extended down an aisle that looked as long as a football field. Most of the coils were neatly stitched up in burlap covers and had obviously never been opened.

Afraid the lode would run out, I scampered over to the next row. There more good fortune awaited. On this row the rope was a size smaller — just what we needed for the stuff higher up. I ordered the watchman to open a few windows in order to get a better look at my bonanza. It turned out better than my wildest hopes. There was plenty of all sizes — more than we could possibly jam into the holds as spare loot . . . .

The watchman seemed to share my enthusiasm. "Ve got more." He led me to the basement. There he showed me thousands of items, all specifically designed for shipboard use. There were bins full of shiny new marlinspikes; there were fids and mallets, turnbuckles, spectacle irons, a generous supply of oakum, tarred hemp of all sizes, and a million wire rope clamps, bolts and shackles. This was a ship rigger's dream.

After wallowing about in my newly found bed of mariner's catnip, I had the watchman seal up the building. On the way back to the ship I stopped in to call on my boss at the Base. With elaborate nonchalance I sidled up to the subject:

"Commodore, may I have a free hand in rounding up stuff necessary for the fitting out of the *Horst Wessel*?"

"Why, yes, McGowan; anybody interfering?"

"No, sir. I think, considering the *Horst Wessel*'s rig, I ought to have some sort of priority when I discover stuff, seeing as how it's going to be so hard to find things we must have. For instance, one of my officers has whipped out a slide rule and estimated that we need twenty-two miles of line just to replace worn-out stuff; and to call the ship seaworthy, there ought to be an ample supply in the bosun's locker and hawser room."

"As much as that?"

"Well, it may not be exact, but it's beginning to look like it will take that much."

"You have a free hand. Take anything you can find within reason. Good hunting!"

Sails, Electronics, and Other Ship's Stores. Commander McGowan's supply officer was German-born and had been brought to the United States when he was twelve years old. His assignment to Germany on the ship's project soon had his natal tongue in working order, and though McGowan does not reveal the officer's full name (in fact, he reveals very few names in the book), his nickname "Von" probably indicates German aristocracy, a theory reinforced by overheard villagers, who called him "Graf," meaning Count. Whatever his background, this partly anonymous young man was an extraordinarily effective scrounger, gifted at extracting information and resources from the exhausted towns and countryside, and he was soon given a free hand, complete discretion in his multifarious searches and seizures. Thousands of objects of both direct and possible use to the ship poured in. Many miles inland, he located a storehouse holding 9,000 yards of flax sailcloth. A week later, he found all the sail twine necessary to sew the sails. When Germany's only remaining working sailmaking guild was discovered to be nearly frozen, starving, and unable to work, "Von" located a truckload of food and, even more mysteriously, a load of stove fuel. When finally the vessel's electrical system had to receive attention, sure enough, the officer chased down rumors, ending at a secret passage under a decrepit shed, a sealed door behind which a large store of new electrical supplies lay hidden. Last but not least, as *Eagle*'s commissioning day approached, white paint appeared, enough for a full coat, and more to stow away. Most of this young man's tale is not told, but *Eagle* must forever be in his debt.

Eagle's original figurehead was removed, lent to Mystic Seaport Museum in Mystic, Connecticut, and later returned for display at the Coast Guard Academy Museum. A duplicate figurehead was made and cast in fiberglass — here shown on display at the Academy's Visitor's Pavilion. The figurehead that today graces Eagle's *bow was carved in the winter of 1975– 76 and placed on the ship the following spring.*

Yard Work and Crew. When Commander McGowan found the ship, all about him was strange, as well as highly distressed, and in witness to the latent international fellowship among mariners, a genuine sense of mutual respect, sympathy, even friendship soon grew between the American commandeering party and the attendant Germans, both on board the ship and at dockside in the nearby Rickmer's Werft shipyard. Until *Eagle* was formally turned over to the Coast Guard by the Navy Department, McGowan in fact had no formal command; indeed the German (former) commanding officer of the ship still occupied the captain's quarters, American billets being ashore in Bremen. Yet, as the weeks and months passed, slowly but surely a sound trust and mutual reliance infused the project. The German crew turned to for every task, not only with the precision and thoroughness in which they had been trained, but also in a spirit of helpfulness, explaining problems and techniques across the language barrier as best they could.

For five generations part of an internationally famous shipyard, the Rickmer's people soon became completely helpful, very candid in their desire to reestablish their reputation and standing in a world that had been turned upside-down. A moving expression of this feeling occurred one day when the family foreman presented a circular plaque to the ship, a United States Coast Guard emblem that perfectly fit the socket held in the talons of the ship's eagle figurehead — a socket that a few months before

The first journey home. With mixed Coast Guard and German crew, Captain McGowan and willing companions bring the ship to home waters through a hurricane off Bermuda. Eagle here is under ordinary full press of canvas. (U.S. Coast Guard Archives photo)

had housed a swastika. When finally the ship was hauled out to be cleaned and painted (and also to have her bomb-damaged rudderpost straightened), McGowan mentions, American and German pride in the ship's beauty and their collective accomplishment were indistinguishable.

How actually to sail the ship across the Atlantic became a nagging problem. Every operation on the vessel, save turning the propeller, producing electricity, and purifying seawater, was manual. After all, the ship was built to carry 220 cadets, 125 enlisted men, and 14 officers — manpower was never foreseen to be a problem. Just to operate the manual anchor capstan required 40 men. Doing that, and managing nearly 22,000 square feet of sail area, seemed out of the question. McGowan had ten men, and as it turned out, from a back-home environment where Americans were jumping out of uniform, the Coast Guard could in good conscience send only another 30 personnel to Germany to help man the ship. The commander was able to recruit a hodge-podge half-score friends and associates to swell the complement, but still the number was too small for basic management, let alone safety. Under constant admonishment, all the Americans had studied the complex rigging of the ship and drilled with it time and time again, and most of the nameplates that infested the ship had been translated into English. Still, the human prospects for a voyage fell short.

McGowan one day fell into conversation with another unnamed associate, a British officer who, it turned out, was in charge of German recruitment in the North Sea minesweeping effort, with authority to hire at will up to a thousand German personnel. In one conversation and a few days' bureaucratic juggling, the ship's German complement became "minesweeping" personnel, officially billeted aboard a lovely white barque, soon to be commissioned *Eagle*.

She was commissioned May 15, 1946. The commodore from the United States Naval Command was piped aboard. American crew stood at attention to starboard, German crew to port. The commander read his orders and stepped into command, quickly ordering the making of the colors, and the new watch was set. The ceremony lasted only a few minutes.

Two weeks later *Eagle* sailed for the United States. She was ten years old. That was forty years ago.

3 A Walking Tour of *Eagle*

Ships are called ships, or vessels, when they are large enough to carry boats, which in turn are called boats when they are small enough to be practically carried by a ship. In the Great Age of Sail, the word *ship* was often reserved specifically for a kind of rig — a three-masted setup, all three masts carrying square sails. The famous clipper ships were *ship* rigged. Other kinds of sail arrangements were designated according to the number of masts they carried, the height and location of their masts, and the kinds of sails and combinations of sails they carried on each mast. These combinations resulted in different names for differing types of vessels.

As the nineteenth century drew to conclusion, many types of sailing rigs began to disappear; indeed the sails themselves began to disappear as reliable steam and internal-combustion plants were devised, and so the word *ship* more and more became a generic name. Properly speaking, the ship *Eagle* is a bark, or, in the current latinate spelling, a *barque,* a term that usually refers to a vessel of any length, with three masts (although the term can be applied to a "four-masted barque"), all of which except the aftermost, which is also the shortest, are fully square-rigged.

Square-rigged refers both to the shape of the sails and the way in which they are attached or bent to their spars; and in ordinary nautical parlance the name is applied in opposition to, or compared to, vessels that are rigged exclusively fore-and-aft. Because barque *Eagle* has both square sails and fore-and-aft sails, we will need some definitions of sail technology.

Masts and Standing Rigging

All sailing boats and ships have at least one mast, usually added to as vessel size increases. Vessels with up to seven masts were built in the past. Attached to the masts are *spars* of various kinds, usually rounded timbers or steel members, to which the sails are bent. When these spars and sails

(U.S. Navy photo by
Duane I. Hansen)

Photography has its place, but something in the artist's vision affects the mind when the subject is rendered in pen and ink. Some things are left out, others included in a way that only the heart knows. (Yngve Soderberg, artist; reproduction courtesy of U.S. Coast Guard Academy Museum)

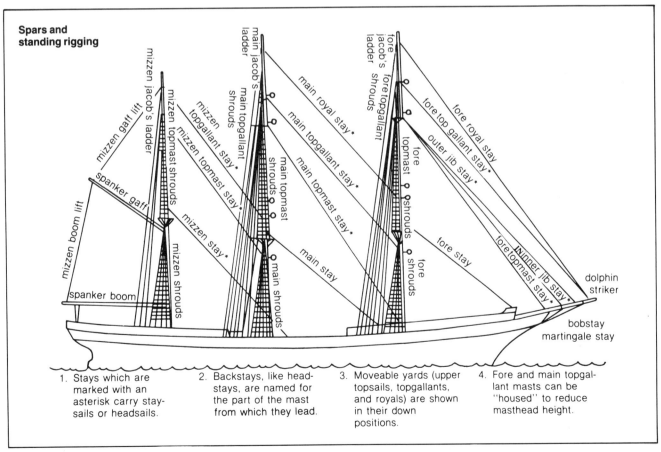

Spars and standing rigging

1. Stays which are marked with an asterisk carry staysails or headsails.

2. Backstays, like headstays, are named for the part of the mast from which they lead.

3. Moveable yards (upper topsails, topgallants, and royals) are shown in their down positions.

4. Fore and main topgallant masts can be "housed" to reduce masthead height.

are attached along the length of a vessel's midline, longitudinally, then they are said to be rigged fore-and-aft. When the spars and sails are rigged across the ship, usually with rectilinear sail shapes, the arrangement is said to be square-rigged. As a barque, *Eagle* has both kinds, and our walking tour of the ship begins aloft, with the vessel's spars, rigging, and sails.

The whole of *Eagle*'s rigging is generally referred to as the *tophamper*, which is held up by three masts and the bowsprit, which in turn are held in place and supported by standing rigging. Moving from the front of the ship, at the bow, to the back of the ship, at the stern, the masts and spars are, respectively, the bowsprit — the steel member that protrudes over the water, off the top of the bow; the foremast, the forward-most vertical member of the rig; the mainmast, at amidships; and finally the mizzen-mast, the strictly fore-and-aft rigged member that rises from the deck, aft.

These mast spars are permanently supported by miles of standing rigging, for the most part of galvanized iron cable wire that makes down from key locations on the masts, to either side of the ship, or to other masts, or to the bowsprit. Pieces of standing rigging that are fixed fore-and-aft are stays, and those which are fixed across, or athwartships, are shrouds. Both stays and shrouds are designated by the place *from which* they make down to other parts of the rigging or ship, though nomenclature sometimes favors a sail they carry. A full explanation of *Eagle*'s spars and standing rigging could entail a baroque symphony of words, and so we invite a visit to the rigging diagrams. As you can see, some complications of nomenclature arise when you consider pieces of standing rigging that make down severely both fore-and-aft and athwartships, such as the backstays. Nevertheless, the general rule is that all rigging is first designated by its mast, then its relative position on the mast, and then its primary function, whether it is to support the mast laterally (shrouds), or fore-and-aft (stays). The ship has a lot of these, and their complexity is enhanced because most of them are, in turn, wormed, served, and parceled by further miles of marlin and oiled-canvas wrapping, which protect them from the corrosive effects of the salt-water environment in which they work.

It is impressive that the Coast Guard's very high safety standards for rigging finds much of *Eagle*'s original cable standing rigging, installed in Hamburg, Germany fifty years ago, still well within its specifications for strength and safety. The best went into her at the beginning, and the finest care has been lavished since. Consider the force of wind on more than 21,000 square feet of sail, driving nearly 2,000 tons of ship, sometimes at nearly seventeen knots (almost twenty miles an hour), for fifty years; it must have been the best.

The Spars and Sails

This splendid orchestration of steel and cable is of course devoted to harnessing the power of the barque, its sails, of which it has two kinds, the fore-and-aft sails and the square sails. For the most part, *Eagle*'s fore-and-

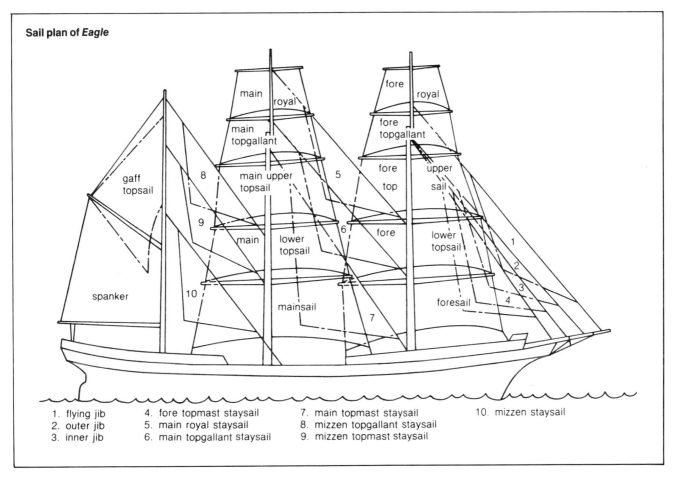

Sail plan of *Eagle*

gaff topsail

spanker

main royal

main topgallant

main upper topsail

main

main lower topsail

mainsail

8

9

10

5

6

7

fore royal

fore topgallant

fore upper top sail

fore

fore lower topsail

foresail

1

2

3

4

1. flying jib	4. fore topmast staysail	7. main topmast staysail	10. mizzen staysail
2. outer jib	5. main royal staysail	8. mizzen topgallant staysail	
3. inner jib	6. main topgallant staysail	9. mizzen topmast staysail	

aft sails are hanked to stays; that is, they are affixed in such a way that they can be hoisted or doused up and down the stays on which they are attached by hanks. Again moving from forward to after parts of the ship in the diagram, we see first the jibs, or foresails. These are the flying jib, outer jib, inner jib, and foretopmaststaysail, and the four of them provide the ship under way with much of its ability to point up into the wind, and much of the ship's forward torquing movement that is critical to its control and steering. We will speak more about why and how *Eagle* sails as she does later in this chapter.

Moving aft, between foremast and mainmast, and mainmast and mizzen, we find six staysails, each with its position and designation, and contributing its strength of force in the windward ability of the barque. Finally, on the mizzenmast, the only strictly fore-and-aft rigged mast on the ship, are the spanker and the gaff-topsail. Yachtsmen will recognize this arrangement and size of sail as that familiar on very large schooners, though *Eagle*'s size renders it relatively diminutive here. Whereas on a strictly fore-and-aft rigged ship *Eagle*'s spanker would provide a large portion of the ship's drive, aboard *Eagle* its primary function is to balance the ship, to provide the after-torquing moment necessary to balance the jibs in sailing to windward, when wind strikes the vessel forward of

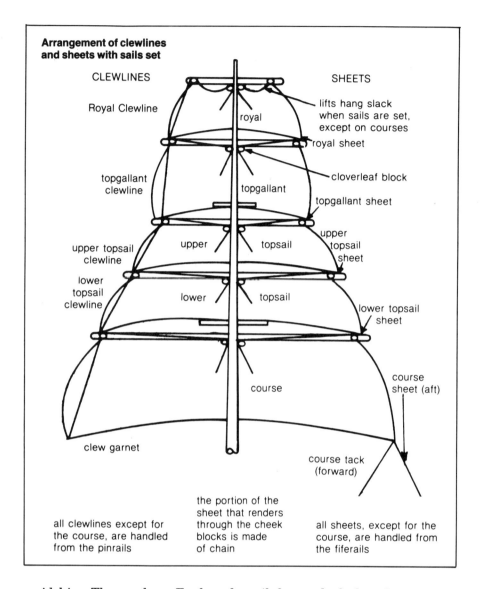

**Arrangement of clewlines
and sheets with sails set**

CLEWLINES   SHEETS

Royal Clewline

royal

lifts hang slack
when sails are set,
except on courses

royal sheet

topgallant
clewline

topgallant

cloverleaf block

topgallant sheet

upper
topsail
sheet

upper topsail
clewline

upper   topsail

lower
topsail
clewline

lower   topsail

lower topsail
sheet

course

course
sheet (aft)

clew garnet

course tack
(forward)

the portion of the
sheet that renders
through the cheek
blocks is made
of chain

all clewlines except for
the course, are handled
from the pinrails

all sheets, except for the
course, are handled from
the fiferails

amidships. Thus we have *Eagle* under sail, fore-and-aft along her midline.

Eagle's most extraordinary character, however, is expressed in her square sails, bent to yards, which cross her foremast and mainmast. As for the pieces of standing rigging, the square sails are designated by their mast and their relative location on each mast. By tradition, they are, from bottom to top, called the foresail (foremost), the mainsail (mainmast), the lower and upper topsails, the topgallants, and the royals. In earlier years of sail a host of other kinds of sails were used aboard square-riggers: sky sails and moon sails (above the royals), studding sails (outside of the square sails), ringtails (aft of the spanker), and even square sails under the bowsprit, called "Jamie-Greens." But all these sails were impractical man-killers, even if they did provide an extra knot or two when the wind was light.

Though she is a square-rigger, *Eagle* is nevertheless a very modern sailing ship, at the peak of sail technology from the close of the sail era.

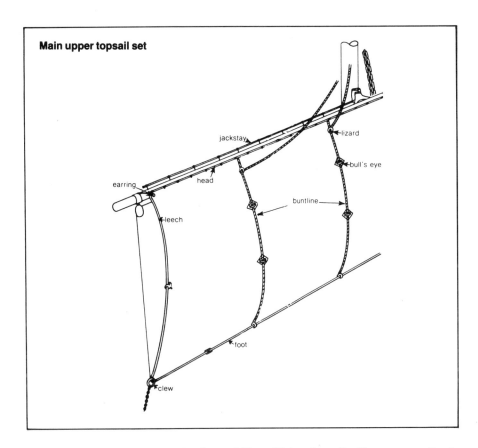

Main upper topsail set

Just realize that 295-foot *Eagle could* be efficiently sailed by a crew of only twenty sailors, but a full-rigged clipper ship, say, of 1840, with half the length and tonnage of *Eagle*, required fifty seamen. Prints and paintings of the old clippers are common, and next time you see one, just imagine having to furl one of the topsails in a breeze of wind in winter. The age of "wooden ships and iron men" is gratefully replaced by steel ships and cherished (though not coddled) cadets at the Coast Guard Academy. Even at that, the mass of *Eagle*'s spars, added to the sheer physics of the wind's force on the sail surfaces, will give pause to any engineering mind.

All these spars and sails must be controlled with utmost reliability and integrity, by means of running rigging, of which *Eagle* possesses five miles. This is the working stuff of the ship, the hands-on means by which mortals can turn the extraordinary latent powers of the wind to their will, if they understand marlinspike seamanship — an ancient term used to designate all the nautical arts as they apply to rope and lines. A crux of *Eagle*'s value as a cadet-training vessel resides in the special way in which sails must be handled, and the greater part of this handling requires understanding and using the running rigging.

Again, most of the detail that needs explanation is best shown rather than described, but common sense makes the elements of sail control straightforward. First, the wind pushes against anything and everything it strikes. Second, sails are designed so as to lead the wind that strikes them to push in a controllable manner. Third, this necessary control has

The main sail

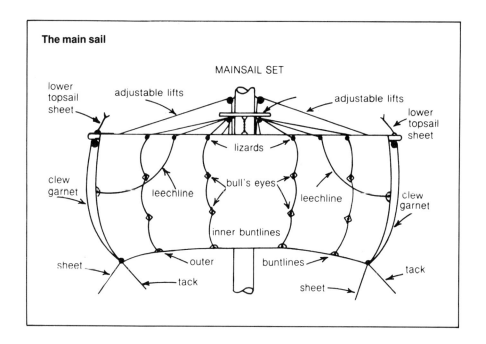

MAINSAIL SET

lower topsail sheet

adjustable lifts

adjustable lifts

lower topsail sheet

lizards

clew garnet

leechline

bull's eyes

leechline

clew garnet

inner buntlines

sheet

outer

buntlines

tack

tack

sheet

Staysail nomenclature

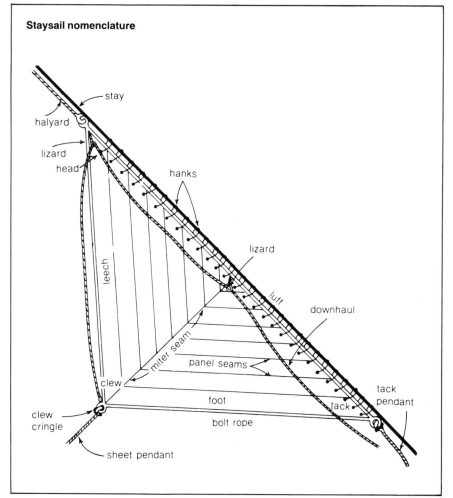

stay

halyard

lizard

head

hanks

lizard

leech

luff

downhaul

miter seam

panel seams

clew

foot

tack

tack pendant

clew cringle

bolt rope

sheet pendant

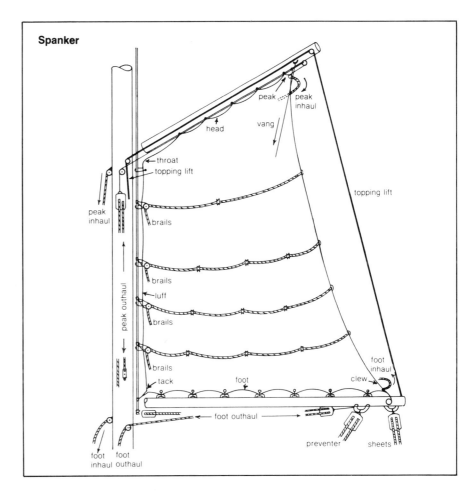

Spanker

mostly to do with how much sail is presented to the wind, and at what angle to the wind; neither too much nor too little sail may be offered to the wind's forces, and the goal is to achieve the most efficient use of the sail area. Running rigging must be able to lift sails (pull them up), to douse sails (pull them down), to bunch them up (to control their bunts, or bellies), and finally, to haul them around at angles that will allow their aspect to the wind to catch close to the wind's full force. In accompanying diagrams, we display and name the parts of *Eagle*'s sails. Each sail comes with myriad small parts and details; each has minutiae explaining attachment to stays and spars; and the fairleading of running rigging hangs hither and yon about the sails, directing sail control to the deck, where work is both safer and easier.

Pieces of running rigging that lift sails are called halyards. Lines that douse sails are called downhauls. Rigging that bunches up sails consists of clew lines, leech lines, and bunt lines. And lines that control the sail's angle of attack toward the wind are either sheets, which haul spars and their sails aft, or braces, which haul spars or sails forward. Other sorts of running rigging, such as preventers, vangs, and outhauls have their places, but those we list are the basics; again, they are designated by the spars and sails that they manipulate. Whole volumes are devoted to the

Pinrail diagram fore castle

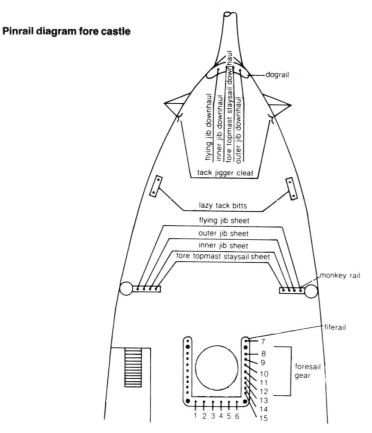

Key
1. fore royal sheet
2. main royal staysail downhaul
3. gantline
4. main topmast staysail downhaul
5. main topgallant staysail downhaul
6. fore royal sheet
7. lower topsail sheet
8. clew garnet
9. fore lift
10. fore leechline
11. fore inner buntline
12. fore outer buntline
13. upper topsail sheet
14. topgallant sheet
15. spare

Pinrail diagram waist, forward

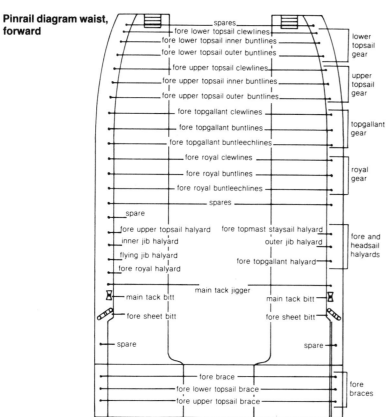

Key
1. spare
2. spare
3. spare
4. main topmast staysail sheet
5. main topgallant staysail sheet
6. main royal staysail sheet
7. spare
8. main lower topsail clewline
9. main lower topsail inner buntline
10. main lower topsail outer buntline
11. main upper topsail clewline
12. main upper topsail inner buntline
13. main upper topsail outer buntline
14. main topgallant clewline
15. main topgallant buntline
16. main topgallant buntleechline
17. main royal clewline
18. main royal buntline
19. main royal buntleechline
20. spare
21. spare
22. main topmast staysail halyard
23. spare
24. fore topgallant brace
25. fore royal brace
26. main topgallant halyard
27. spare
28. main royal staysail halyard
29. main upper topsail sheet
30. main outer buntline
31. main inner buntline
32. main leechline
33. main lift
34. main clew-garnet
35. main royal sheet
36. gantline
37. mizzen topmast staysail downhaul
38. mizzen staysail downhaul
39. mizzen topgallant staysail downhaul
40. main royal sheet
41. main upper topsail halyard
42. main topgallant staysail halyard
43. main royal halyard

Key
1. staysail sheet
2. topmast staysail sheet
3. topgallant staysail sheet
4. gaff topsail sheet
5. spare
6. gaff topsail clew
7. timenoguy
8. topgallant staysail halyard
9. spare
10. main topgallant brace
11. main royal brace
12. main brace
13. main lower topsail brace
14. main upper topsail brace
15. brails
16. main staysail halyard
17. foot inhaul
18. foot outhaul
19. topsail tack
20. topping fit
21. peak inhaul
22. peak outhaul
23. topsail tack
24. gaff topsail halyard
25. topmast staysail halyard

Pinrail diagram waist, aft

Pinrail diagram mizzenmast

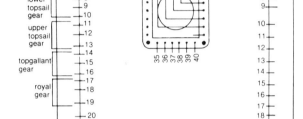

hulls and rigging of sailing ships; some of the classics and current books on the subject are listed in the bibliography.

With some exceptions, the running rigging leads down to the deck, where each line is affixed to belaying pins; these are specially shaped shafts of either bronze or wood (oak or black locust) that line the rails around the perimeter of the ship, or come down to fife rails, which are railed sets of belaying pins that surround the base of each mast at about waist height above the deck. Although some few of these are used only once in a while, aboard *Eagle* 202 pins stand by, and this number does not include the many cleats and bits on and around the deck and spars, to which lines are made fast under special circumstances. Not only does the vessel have to tie up with many lines to moor at docks and wharves, she also has her own boats aboard, requiring their own davit gear and attendant holdfasts; and all manner of facilities for warping to, managing ground tackle (anchor), towing other vessels, managing cargo and gangways, and so on, are available, involving running rigging or near relations. To be a proper sailing ship, hundreds of contingencies must be planned for and supplied with facilities. Many of these involve pieces of rope, or lines, and every one of them needs: (1) to be available where it is to be applied; (2) a place in which to be stored or set; (3) complete understanding about its purpose and use; and (4) a ready procedure for its use. The ship's company must be ever mindful of the five miles of fibrous lines.

None of this rope could do its job without many types of fittings designed and installed to attach, guide, lead, and protect both the standing and the running rigging of the ship. Everywhere are fairleads (usually metal rings affixed to spars, deck, or hull to lead pieces of rigging away from places where they will chafe or wear against something else), lizards (round tropical-hardwood rings on the end of standing parts of running rigging that act either as fairleads or as passive blocks), and bullseyes (fairleads sewn into the cloth of the sails). And then, thimbles, shackles, and blocks of all kinds and sizes are the metal fixtures employed in attaching, protecting, and guiding the many lines in their multifaceted business. Just as ashore, at sea on sailing vessels a thousand gadgets, gilhinkies, and wrinkles confront cadets, who must come to know and understand them and learn the subtle details that make better mariners and officers, in capacities far removed from sail.

Eagle's Hull

Everyone who sees her knows instinctively that *Eagle* is beautiful. Yachtsmen and marine enthusiasts have many names describing parts of a ship with which they explain why the ship is good or not so good, beautiful or less than perfect. As for the rigging, entire dictionaries are devoted to forms, parts, and parcels of ships. So that we can soon walk through our ship, we will remain with the basics.

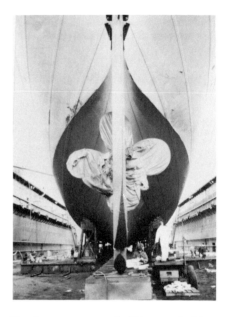

Eagle's curvaceous hull is revealed by her "body plan." The ship's forebody is shown on the right side of the drawing, her afterbody on the left side. Above and below, Eagle is shown in dry-dock, stern-on and bow-on. Once every two years the ship is hauled out for inspection, cleaning, replacement of the zincs (zinc metal plates attached to the hull to prevent electrolytic corrosion), and painting. The vessel's eight-foot-diameter propellor is kept under wraps to protect it from paint and haphazard damage. (Ed Daniels photos)

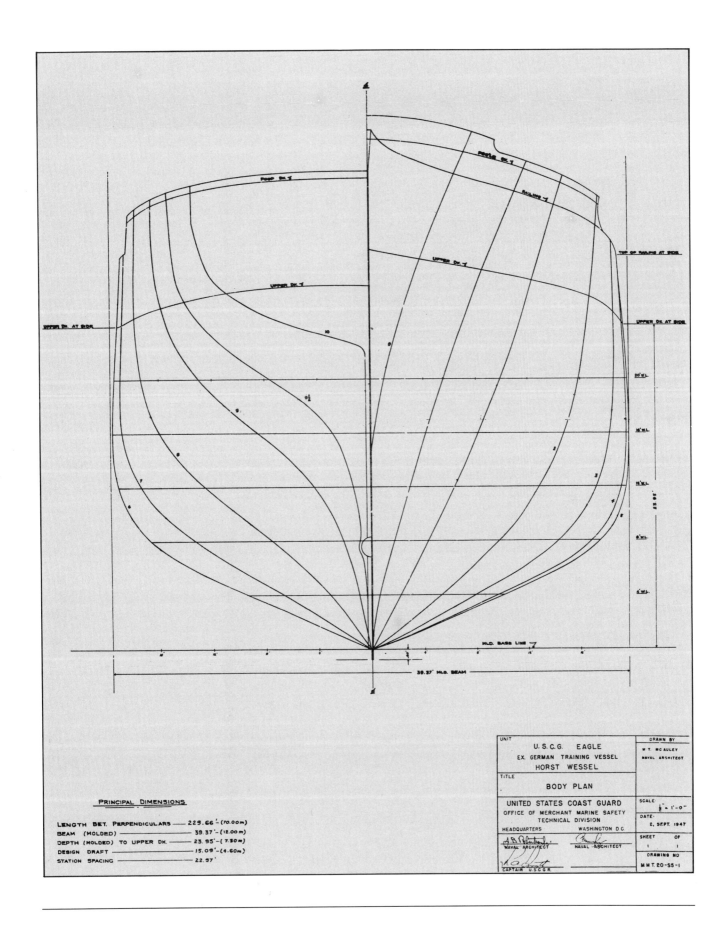

PRINCIPAL DIMENSIONS

LENGTH BET. PERPENDICULARS ——— 229.66' - (70.00 m)
BEAM (MOLDED) ——————————— 39.37' - (12.00 m)
DEPTH (MOLDED) TO UPPER DK. ——— 23.95' - (7.30 m)
DESIGN DRAFT ————————————— 15.09' - (4.60 m)
STATION SPACING —————————— 22.97'

UNIT		DRAWN BY
U. S. C. G. EAGLE EX. GERMAN TRAINING VESSEL HORST WESSEL		W. T. MCAULEY NAVAL ARCHITECT
TITLE		
BODY PLAN		
UNITED STATES COAST GUARD OFFICE OF MERCHANT MARINE SAFETY TECHNICAL DIVISION	SCALE: ½" = 1'-0"	
	DATE: 2 SEPT. 1947	
HEADQUARTERS WASHINGTON D.C. NAVAL ARCHITECT NAVAL ARCHITECT CAPTAIN U.S.C.G.R.	SHEET OF 1 1	
	DRAWING NO MMT 20-S5-1	

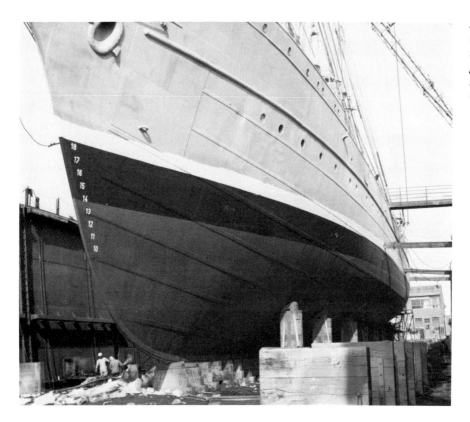

A "three-quarter" view of Eagle's *underbody in dry-dock shows the ship's fine hydrodynamic surfaces — graceful lines that make 2000 tons of ship into a thoroughbred.* (U.S. Coast Guard Academy photo)

The overall mass of the ship is called its hull. Its weight, everything of which the vessel is made, everything on it and in it, combines to make up its displacement, meaning that when she sits at her lines, floating, she displaces a weight of water exactly equal to her tonnage. Looking at the ship from afar we see her topsides, sweeping in a graceful sheer line along her deck and bulwarks, from her fine clipper bow and figurehead, to her curved and carving-emblazoned counterstern. Below the water line and out of ordinary sight, the ship's long, straight keel allows her to track well, to stay on course with minimal correction of steering and sideslip through the water as the vessel heels under the enormous wind forces aloft. The bottom of the ship is a massive compound-complex curvilinear surface sweeping up into firm, round bilges, on which the ship bears when under sail, and aft along a smooth and gentle run, so that the ship moves easily and efficiently through the water. Aft of everything, *Eagle*'s great rudder makes down along the rudderpost, to the keel of the ship. Controlled by two steering stations on deck, most notably the triple-wheeled helm on the bridge deck, the rudder guides the vessel by interrupting the flow of water as it nears the stern, pushing the stern one way or the other and so altering the course of the ship.

The deck is a paradigm of form serving function. About most of the rail, and at each mast partner where masts and deck meet, belaying-pin rails secure the ship's running-rigging. Up forward, on the ship's raised fore-deck superstructure, much of the business is devoted to ground tackle, the capstans and bits used to power, control, and finally hold *Eagle*'s anchor

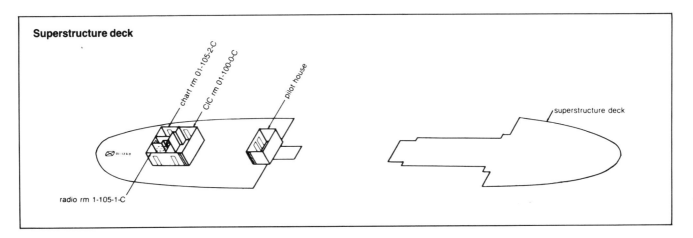

Superstructure deck

chart rm 01-105-2-C

CIC rm 01-100-0-C

pilot house

01-125-0

superstructure deck

radio rm 1-105-1-C

chains. Composed of 140 fathoms (6 feet to a fathom) of 1.75-inch chain, each chain terminates at large patent anchors, the "Navy" anchor to port of 3,500 pounds, the German anchor (one of the ship's originals) to starboard of 3,800 pounds. Although since 1954 *Eagle* has had powerful electric winches to hoist the enormous weight of these anchors and their chains, there once was in their place an old-fashioned man-powered capstan, now in storage in Baltimore. The capstan brings to mind the sea-chanteys sung by seamen to ease the endless walk around and around this notoriously tedious device.

Under way, at least two cadets are posted on the foredeck at all times. One is a lookout who stays in the eyes of the ship at the forepeak, and the other is a talker, an assistant lookout who via head-mounted intercom remains in continuous communication with the traffic monitor in the pilot house on the bridge. The after portion of the foredeck, aft of the foremast, is a runway of sorts, formerly the stowage site for the ship's motor launch and captain's gig; these days the ship's automatically inflating liferaft capsules nest here, along with the gallows post for the cargo boom. Overall, the foredeck is an ideal place for general observation of the sea and ship's business, out of harm's way and not especially busy, except of course during ground-tackle regimes and sail drills.

Amidships is the waist deck. *Eagle*'s status as a training ship is given away in part by a relatively short waist deck, and comparatively long fore and after superstructures. Commercial sailing barques had very small raised decks and very long waists, which, when the ships were fully laden with cargo, would often be awash with boarding seas. *Eagle,* when pressed in a breeze, will occasionally put her deck edge under as water surges through her freeing ports, but not often. Young cadets, a full career from being shellbacks, have quite enough to do and think about without aqueous hazards threatening on deck.

The waist is perhaps the most polyfunctional place aboard. Fully half of the running rigging runs down to it. Being most out of the weather while under way, it is also the place where much of the vessel's portable bo's'n's work is accomplished — overhauling gear, painting equipment, marlinspike work, and airing and drying nearly everything prone to wetness. At other times it becomes a parade ground, site of ship's musters, daily and full-dress inspections, and special ceremonial and recreational events, and quite often it is used as a gymnasium. When other matters are not pressing here, the off watch commonly works out in the waist, and small highjinks are not unknown.

To either side of the engine room's fiddley, a deck housing that pierces all below-decks to the engine room, are two companionways leading to the afterdeck superstructure, which is divided up from fore to aft into the bridge — an area of general purview and command made up of the pilot house, wings, ready-boat area, and the helm. Aft of this section is the chart house and radio-shack structure, with waterway decks on either side, and finally, aft of the chart house, is the poop deck, dominated by the manual warping capstan and emergency wheel and its coffin. The very aftermost terminus of the poop is usually referred to as the fantail by those with either naval or strictly power-cutter experience in the service.

From the point of view of authority and command, the bridge is the heart of the ship. It is here that the Commanding Office (CO) or Officer of the Deck (OOD) usually wield authority, and where those most in possession of information about the vessel's situation and condition coordinate their knowledge and skills. The pilot house, a tiny steel structure, holds a radar unit, lookout-contact post, and traffic-monitoring station to port, and a small piloting station to starboard, the two areas divided by a complex of inner-ship communication units mounted on a bulkhead that houses the main-drive plant's exhaust stack. With constant interchange between the situation and traffic personnel to port, and the continuous dead-reckoning and course monitoring to starboard, often with lookers-on and cooperating cadets at study in both areas, the pilot house is a hotbed of organized turmoil 'round the clock.

Just aft of the pilot house is the helm, composed of the binnacle (which houses the ship's primary magnetic steering compass), an engine-control telegraph, and *Eagle*'s mighty triple wheel. The boat's winch is also here. This is not a modest place. When you step up onto the raised teak grating that surrounds the helm, grasp the wheel at one or another of its six stations, and gaze about — ahead at the compass, above the pilot house at the rudder-position indicator, and all about at the informed authority — you cannot deny the feeling of both control and responsibility. Further-more, *Eagle* is a responsive sailing vessel, and what you do here is immedi-ately reflected in the ship's responses.

On either side of the helm are the lifeboats, rigged and ready for immedi-ate use. These double-ended power boats not only replace the lifeboats of yore, but they vastly expand the utility and capability of *Eagle* as an instructional vessel and as an effective cutter in the Coast Guard Service. These boats are extraordinarily able. Few days at sea do not see one or both launched to perform standard drills in their use. After all, most Coast Guard personnel, most of the time, are either serving in small craft, or tending to the activities and welfare of small craft. These are lifeboats, but they are also much, much more, and their launching, retrieval, and man-agement alongside a sailing vessel, *under way*, form a tricky and fascinating task. Business must go on as usual on the bridge at all times, and so the potential for confusion, the demand for order, and the intense activity during boat drills on the bridge deck are exciting beyond imagination. To see *Eagle*'s small boats bounding about the seas on the open ocean around the vessel while she is on course, sails drawing, is a compelling vision. It is a certainty that these drills will one day save lives.

Aft of the bridge, the chart house dominates, as the largest deck structure. To have ten or a dozen personnel pursuing their errands in the chart house all at once is not unusual. With its own mostly navigational facilities, and its separately enclosed radio-communications shack, it is the most sophisticated entity on the ship, incongruous though it is with the ship's primary means of locomotion. Here resides the vessel's primary (sixty-mile range-scan) radar; a radio direction finder; a radar situation scenario-generation scope; both digital- and paper-recording depth sounders; and satellite navigation (SAT-NAV), OMNI, and LORAN units, all capable of accurately rendering the ship's position anywhere on the world's oceans to within a few score yards of certainty. As a cadet trainer, *Eagle* must also sponsor pencil-and-paper navigation techniques, based on visual sunshots with the sextant. As a fully commissioned Coast Guard cutter, she must carry state-of-the-art equipment, as well.

The radio room is part of the chart house, and here too the relatively ancient visual techniques join the most modern communication facilities. Communications officers are trained in the whole gamut of message-transmission techniques, from visual Morse and signal-flag clusters, to encoded radio transmission and reception, teletype, and weatherfax equipment. *Eagle* uses and trains personnel in using all of it. Messages come and go regularly, mostly in communication with the Coast Guard Academy in New London, local District Headquarters, and nearby vessels and aircraft.

The afterdeck or poop deck of the ship is taken up mostly by the great coffin housing the steering gear. With just one wheel, this unit is directly connected to the rudderpost and is used only when the regular three-wheeled unit on the bridge is being overhauled or repaired. Cushioned seating lines the splendidly varnished coffin housing, and it is here that ship's guests and host officers often congregate to watch the seas passing and to talk. Just aft of this area, the deck ends at the taffrail, where, in the midst of the spanker boom's sheet, stern lookouts are stationed on watch at the rail, again with a talker in constant communication with the bridge. Overlooking the ship's wake and the sea life that often feeds in the wake's churning waters, this can be a contemplative spot, an out-of-the-way place for thoughts about ships, their people, and the sea.

For the relatively great size of *Eagle*, the large complement of ship's personnel, and the constant hum of activity in which it engages, few bulkhead hatches (doorways) provide access to the ship's labyrinthine interior. Of the nine, only five are regularly used. The reason for this dearth of access is safety: fewer hatches make it harder for water to enter the ship. These massive steel polylevered and latched doors are designed with great strength and watertight integrity.

In Chapter 2 we described the theory behind the vessel's transverse-

Main deck

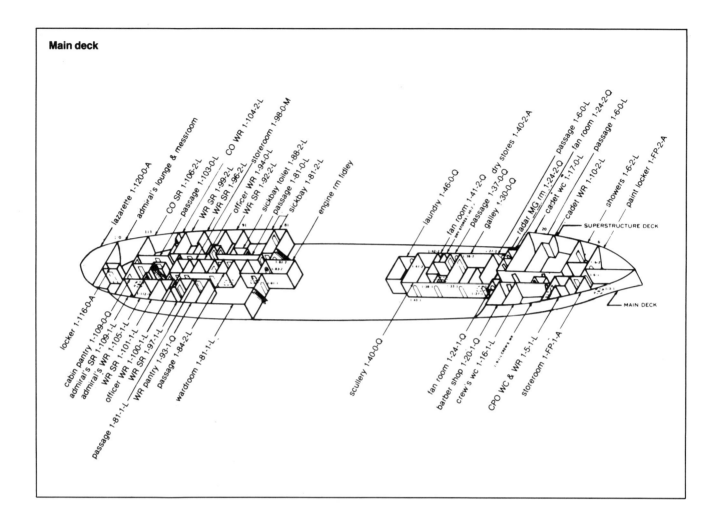

framing system, supplying much of the ship's strength by means of the deck structures, rather than massive vertical framing inside the skin of the ship. This method of construction saves greatly in hull weight, an advantage for a sailing ship, which needs more weight in ballast; it also makes more room below, an excellent characteristic for a training vessel that must provide ambient areas for people rather than inert cargo space. With a deck length of 277 feet, a breadth of 39 feet, and a draft of 17 feet, *Eagle* has a highly complex area below, with divisions providing for an enormous range of activities and facilities. Deck by deck, our exploration continues.

Being a primary structural member, the waist deck is but an open-air appearance of a deck that in fact continues under the superstructures from one end of the ship to the other. Moving forward from amidships, where a large housing divides the deck into port and starboard waterways (relatively narrow decks that are port and starboard continuations of the waist decks forward), the aftermost house section is given over to one-third of the primary domestic necessities (after eating and sleeping), laundry. What do you do to provide for 150 to 200 very active shipboard personnel, who are expected both to do hard physical work and to appear for full-dress military

The flag dining cabin. Here the commanding officer of Eagle *and embarked dignitaries take their repasts.* (U.S. Coast Guard Academy photo by Doug Bandos)

inspection regularly? To provide a civilized environment, in which uniforms of the day can be changed several times a day, and sheets and pillowcases never forgone, for weeks at a time at sea, the laundry cabin and its watch-duty detail seldom find idle time.

Forward of the laundry, the ship's scullery, a double companionway leading below, the primary (crew's) galley, and service compartments occupy the rest of the deckhouse. As the deck continues under the foredeck superstructure, these service areas proliferate, in bathrooms (heads), specialized stowage and utility lockers, and the paint locker, storing some of the volatiles used aboard ship in isolated and ventilated safety.

When *Eagle* was first brought into United States service, Commander McGowan says, the ship's galley was simply two open burners and two very large kettle-pot units, presumably used for the usual German navy fare of soups and sauerkraut. *Eagle's* contemporary galleys offer the full range of modern American diet, eclectic and often creative. The three galleys are the main crew-mess galley, the wardroom galley, and the small, special captain's galley, devoted to special fare at special times. Food aboard the ship is excellent and offered in bounty — cadets are young, healthy, and extremely active in the sea air. They eat well and a lot, making a separate galley for the officers in the wardroom almost mandatory for the older, less physically active commissioned personnel. Between the laundry and crew-mess galley, the scullery is like sculleries through the centuries: a steaming, clattering maelstrom of cleanliness and crew eager to end the watch on this Coast Guard equivalent of KP.

Where the waist-deck portion of the main deck disappears under the after superstructures into officer country, service-oriented spaces continue. Here is the sickbay, a fully equipped clinic for attending to all manner of minor health problems and for stabilizing major illness or trauma until patients can be evacuated. A ship's doctor and a corpsman are always assigned on *Eagle's* cruises. Here, too, are several staterooms assigned to commissioned officers, including the captain and the executive officer. To starboard is the wardroom and its galley, a cabin rather simple in layout and extraordinarily active. In most ways it is headquarters for the plan and spirit of all ship's operations, if not always for the details. Aftermost on this deck, the flag cabin rules. With its own small (and exquisitely productive) galley, and guest VIP sleeping cabin, in this sternmost island of paneled solitude the best-laid plans of the Coast Guard educational system are often presented, and quite often made.

The second deck, too, is a stem-to-stern, integral structural member of the vessel, designed and built specifically to tie the hull together as a unit. Although scores of small bulkheads divide the space into dozens of cabins, this deck can also be thought of as one continuous structural plane, broken in a few places along its midline with small companionways to allow passage to areas above and below.

For the most part, the second deck is given over to sleeping and eating. Forward of amidships are the crew's messroom, the CPOs' mess, and quarters for both. Cadet quarters of several categories are provided here. The largest space, the cadet and crew messrooms (divided by a service

Far aft in the second deck, the ship's office is a hive of activity almost around the clock. Personnel reports and evaluations, plans of the day, ship's requisitions and consumption reports, and publications by the thousands pass through this small hub of intense activity. (U.S. Coast Guard photo by Paula Hobson)

bulkhead), is a site for eating and also for classroom duty, lectures, movies, and shipboard theater. Here below, out of wind and weather, other realities can be portrayed, studied, and observed, usually at an angle as the ship heels in the breeze.

Aft of the mess is the main men's cadet berthing area. The extensive refurbishing of the early 1980s made this a specialized place for sleeping and stowage of personal effects, exclusively. In the old days the entire central second deck was a broad open area, across the beam of the ship, that did double duty for eating and sleeping. The cadets slept in hammocks, which by day were struck, lashed, and stowed to make room for the portable tables that were unfolded and dogged to the deck for eating and, between meals, for study, all in a space without the air conditioning system cadets enjoy today. On this modernized ship, with women fully integrated into the service, and generally higher material expectations among service personnel, berthing areas are divided into special permanent areas, much more comfortable, with fixed-mattress berths. For the crew, sleeping is still cheek-by-jowl, but each cadet now has a personal, if not especially private, space. The ship can provide sleeping accommodations for 240 people, though between 180 and 200 is the usual complement.

Aft of the largest cadet berthing area is a complex of more officer berthing and the ship's office. This is a hotbed of paperwork, monitoring and reporting on every member of the ship's personnel, the vessel's business, sorting out the ship's news, and testing huge quantities of coffee, for gastrointestinal efficacy if not always flavor. Because *Eagle* is both a school and a cutter in its assignments, the ship's office works around the clock, busier even than the ship's laundry, or the galleys.

We decend now to the "first platform," an interrupted deck but a fasci-

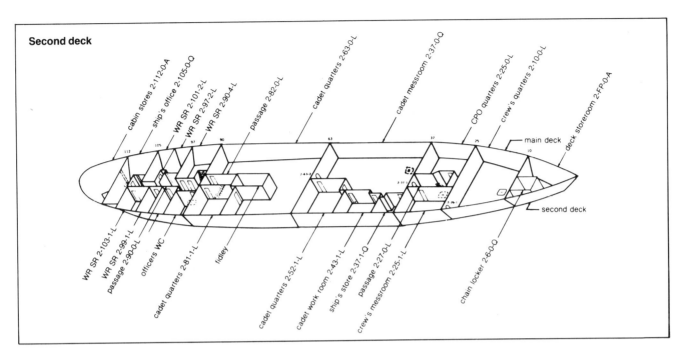

Second deck

cabin stores 2-112-0-A
ship's office 2-105-0-Q
WR SR 2-101-2-L
WR SR 2-97-2-L
WR SR 2-90-4-L
passage 2-82-0-L
cadet quarters 2-63-0-L
cadet messroom 2-37-0-Q
CPO quarters 2-25-0-L
crew's quarters 2-10-0-L
deck storeroom 2-FP-0-A
main deck
second deck

WR SR 2-103-1-L
WR SR 2-99-1-L
passage 2-90-0-L
officers WC
cadet quarters 2-81-1-L
fidley
cadet quarters 2-52-1-L
cadet work room 2-43-1-L
ship's store 2-37-1-Q
passage 2-27-0-L
crew's messroom 2-25-1-L
chain locker 2-6-0-Q

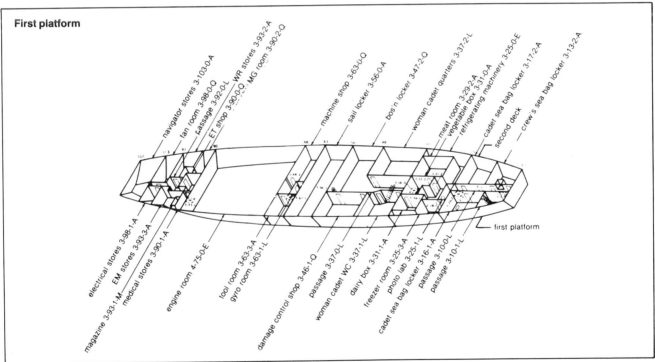

First platform

navigator stores 3-103-0-A
fan room 3-98-0-Q
passage 3-92-0-L
ET shop 3-90-0-Q
WR stores 3-93-2-A
MG room 3-90-2-Q
machine shop 3-63-0-Q
sail locker 3-56-0-A
bos'n locker 3-47-2-Q
woman cadet quarters 3-37-2-L
meat room 3-29-2-A
vegetable box 3-31-0-A
refrigerating machinery 3-25-0-E
cadet sea bag locker 3-17-2-A
crew's sea bag locker 3-13-2-A
second deck
first platform

electrical stores 3-98-1-A
magazine 3-93-1-M
EM stores 3-93-3-A
medical stores 3-90-1-A
engine room 4-75-0-E
tool room 3-63-3-A
gyro room 3-63-1-L
damage control shop 3-46-1-Q
passage 3-37-0-L
woman cadet WC 3-37-1-A
dairy box 3-31-1-A
freezer room 3-25-3-A
photo lab 3-25-1-L
cadet sea bag locker 3-16-1-A
passage 3-10-0-L
passage 3-10-1-L

nating region where a great deal of the ship's business is done. Its fore-section holds yet more stowage and berthing areas and food-freezer compartments.

Amidships are the busy bo's'n's hole and sail lockers, where the endless miles and acres of the ship's lines and sails are both created and overhauled. Here is a fully found woodworking shop, a tool room, and a ma-

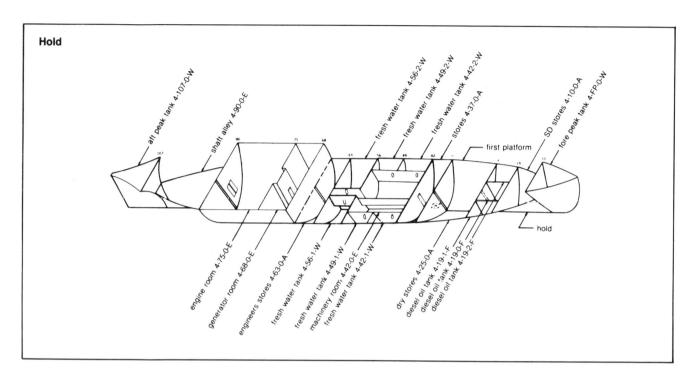

Hold

aft peak tank 4-107-0-W

shaft alley 4-90-0-E

fresh water tank 4-56-2-W

fresh water tank 4-49-2-W

fresh water tank 4-42-2-W

stores 4-37-0-A

SD stores 4-10-0-A

fore peak tank 4-FP-0-W

first platform

hold

engine room 4-75-0-E

generator room 4-68-0-E

engineers stores 4-63-0-A

fresh water tank 4-56-1-W

fresh water tank 4-49-1-W

machinery room 4-42-0-E

fresh water tank 4-42-1-W

dry stores 4-25-0-A

diesel oil tank 4-19-1-F

diesel oil tank 4-19-0-F

diesel oil tank 4-19-2-F

chine shop. Not a tinkerer do-it-yourselfer, let alone a journeyman shop man or woman, in the land would find the materials-handling and crafts sheds of *Eagle* wanting. In these small, relatively cramped below-decks spaces, nearly all the vessel's basic manufacturing needs can be and are met. Rigging and sails are made up all the time; down here, a boat could be built, an engine fabricated from start to finish, were the order received. Nearby is the ship's store, a dispensary for personal supplies and effects and keepsakes bearing the *Eagle* logo. Ordinarily these are available only to the crew and the ship's alumni. A full-rigged sailing barque is operated inexpensively, but not cheaply, and its wares are distributed carefully. *Eagle* caps, tee shirts, and jackets are kept special, just as the ship is.

From here aft, from three fifths of the water line abaft the vessel's cut water (where the bow enters the water), and downward well into the bilges, most of the remaining space is devoted to the engineering department. Some small areas have stowage space for navigation and medical stores; the ship's magazine, where small arms and ammunition are kept; and a gyro room, where the master gyrocompass does its work, sending out its metered readings to a half dozen repeaters on deck. These occupy but a fraction of the area. The rest is composed of the engine room and its contiguous compartments housing the engines, fans, compressors, generators, and pumps that keep *Eagle*'s mechanics and utilities going. The whole area is noisy, and all personnel are required to wear safety ear protection here. A good deal of lip reading, hand signaling, and message scrawling go on in this cacophonous netherworld of the ship.

The main engine is a sixteen-cylinder, 1,000 horsepower, turbocharged Caterpillar diesel that drives the seven-and-one-eighth-inch-diameter shaft and eight-foot-diameter wheel (propeller), moving the ship at a

Eagle's famous and occasionally infamous evaporator, a most desirable if not actually vital machine. Operating properly, it precludes rationing of water on long passages. Desalination burns up most of the fuel used aboard the ship. (U.S. Coast Guard Academy photo by Doug Bandos)

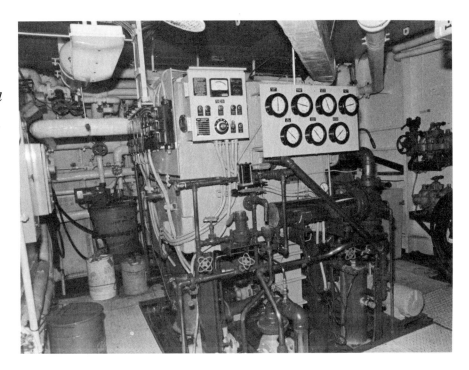

respectable ten-knot cruising speed. This power is relatively new for *Eagle,* whose commanders for many generations of Coast Guard cadets had to be circumspect about maneuvering under power. The original German M.A.N. diesel, of 740 horsepower, was used until 1982; deck commands telegraphed to go from one engine status to another took an averge of forty-eight seconds. Now, with much more power and better engine controls, the ship's operations under power are more positive and more like responses that cadets will experience when they serve on other vessels and craft in Coast Guard service.

At several locations along bilge-bulkhead mountings, auxiliary service and backup engines and motors serve special needs, mostly pumps. Two 225-kilowatt electrical ship's service generators are located in a compartment just forward of the engine room, just to port of where the ship's extraordinary water maker screeches at its duty. Capable of producing 8,000 gallons of fresh water from seawater every 24 hours, it is seldom called upon to do so, but even at modest output it uses most of the fuel consumed aboard the ship, whether or not the main-drive engine is operating at full capacity. The entire ship is ventilated at all times, with air-conditioning in warm months and heat in cool and cold ones — another extensive system of conduits to be supplied and maintained. Finally, 120-volt lines serve every corner of the ship, stem to stern, keel to truck. The engineers have the hot and cold fresh-water systems to heads, sinks, showers, and galleys; the pressure seawater system for fire-suppression outlets; heated or cooled air to scores of cabins and compartments; electrical service to all vital technical stations; and lighting throughout the ship to tend to — they have their hands full, around the clock.

Abaft the main engine room, the shaft alley leads to the mighty stuffing

box, through which thc drive shaft pierces the hull to the propellor. Filling
the dead rise of the counter, where the ship's lines curve down into a
narrow hull section, the aft-peak tank securely holds its trim-ballast water
charge. At the bottom of the ship, its bilges are reserved mostly for tankage, as is the lower section of the forepeak in the bow. Some engineers' and
dry stores are kept here, but *Eagle*'s fresh water and fuel take up the bulk
of the area. Below all the rest where possible, and chocked-in where it must
be, 344 tons of pig-iron ballast is stowed and secured, bringing the ship to
her lines and providing the counterforces required by a sailing vessel —
righting moments that make the ship stand up to wind forces in the
rigging. The lower reaches of the ship are strictly utilitarian, austere, and
often a mass of exposed piping, wiring, and conduits. These are visceral
places, complicated, cramped, often hot, and utterly vital.

The Great Refurbishing

By 1979, *Eagle* had served in continuous duty, year in and year out, ten
years in the German Navy and thirty-three years in the United States
Coast Guard, without a major overhaul. In more than hundreds of thousands of sea miles and forty-three years of oceanic duty, the original ship's
plating, spars, and rigging took their strains, the sea's chemistry worked
its mischief, the same elderly machinery cranked at its duty, and accom-
modation spaces that were thought to be airless in the 1930s were still
thought airless into the century's final quarter. In January 1979, the
Department of Transportation, together with the Coast Guard, surveyed
all training vessels under its jurisdiction, including *Eagle*. Corroded materials, holed decks and bulkheads, and obsolescent machinery were quickly
exposed, and so too was doubt about whether the ship should be kept in
commission, replaced, or repaired. Later in that year an official Ship
Structure Machinery Evaluation Board was convened to conduct and oversee a complete survey of the ship, then to seek second opinions from naval
engineers, and finally to recommend repair guidelines and methods. The
Coast Guard Academy quickly demonstrated how its training criteria and
educational policies required that *Eagle* continue as a vital part in its
programs. With this powerful sentiment behind the effort, an extensive list
of mandatory repairs and replacements and desirable improvements soon
was ready. Very high classification specifications had been laid down by
Germanischer Lloyd, the German counterpart of the famed Lloyds of
London, when the ship was built. The Coast Guard therefore went to the
same German house for a second opinion. All the Coast Guard's findings
and recommendations were soon confirmed, and the German Lloyds raised
the question of stability, for a half century of accumulated repairs,
changes, and modified practices might have altered the ship's righting
moments at some angles of heel and some wind and sea conditions.

The original design criteria for the ship's stability were no longer available, and so the service turned to data created in 1959 when *Gorch Fock II*,

a sister to *Eagle,* underwent inclination experiments to determine her stability. The Coast Guard used these data as the basis on which to set up its own requirements for sailing vessels and sailing auxiliaries carrying passengers, the Merchant Marine Technical intact stability standards, under sail, and the Navy ninety-knot wind-heel criteria, with sails furled.

For her specifications on hull integrity, the Coast Guard applied the standard "Stability and Buoyancy of U.S. Naval Ships," its classification criteria for ships in unrestricted service. The vessel would have to be almost totally stripped from stem to stern, keel to deck, and watertight bulkheads would be added to divide the ship's spaces into many smaller units than formerly. This classification of vessels supplies formulas that determine a vessel's ability to withstand flooding — any encroachment by the sea into the hull's interior. The technique is "compartmentation," which despite the implication that it counts watertight spaces, instead calculates the effects of typical nautical disasters such as ramming, grounding, and explosion. Although she had been built as a one-compartment ship, decades of wear and tear had downgraded her to a zero-compartment vessel, meaning that, in one way or another, water entering the vessel anywhere could eventually get to anywhere else. To bring the ship up to a full two-compartment standard, all decks were either replaced or thoroughly tightened, and nine watertight bulkheads were fixed into the hull. Only a grievous and extraordinary combination of events could sink the barque *Eagle.* In effect, she is now two ships in one.

A full year of institutional fretting and much expert analysis and planning yielded a four-year program of systematic refurbishing for the vessel, conducted in an emergency phase and three annual progressive improvement and modernization phases. The shopping list for the entire program will give pause if one owns a boat. In bare outline, this is the list:

Emergency Phase

a. Replace main weather deck
b. Destructive stay testing, foremast
c. Rivet repair
d. Repair hull, bulkhead, and deck
f. Electrical upgrade
g. Upgrade habitability
h. Replace anchor windlass
i. Renew reefer box
j. Ballast-area preservation
k. Overhaul mainmast
l. Replace watertight doors and hatches

Phase I — Frame 63 Forward

a. Install 3 transverse watertight bulkheads, at frame stations 10, 25, and 49
b. Replace foredeck
c. Renew main deck
d. Renew second deck
e. Upgrade ventilation

Phase II — Frame 63 Aft

a. Install 3 transverse watertight bulkheads
b. Replace poop deck
c. Renew main deck
d. Renew second deck
e. Upgrade ventilation
f. Electrical upgrade

g. Complete furnishing
   replacement
h. Electronic upgrade: collision avoidance, omega
i. Replace chart house
j. 25′ MSB replacement
k. Davit modification
l. Overhaul mizzenmast
m. Replace auxiliary propulsion machinery
n. Replace support
   machinery
o. Replace watertight doors,
   hatches, and fittings

Phase III
a. Teak installation
b. Replace reefer machinery
c. Replace telephone sound-
   powered phone
d. Ballast area preservation
e. Overhaul bowsprit
f. Ventilation improvements
g. Rewire mast and navigation lights

The list is rife with complications, above all because the entire program was not permitted to interrupt *Eagle*'s normal seasonal training schedule. For six months each year she was in dry-dock; for the other six months she was on duty, in service for the cadets.

The vessel was literally torn apart in dry-dock each fall, after her regular sailing season. Furnishings and cosmetic surfaces were removed to expose the structure of the ship and the miles of service piping, wiring, and conduits. With many specialists simultaneously working at their tasks, on a tight schedule, to complete the hundreds of jobs in each winter season, frustrations struck at the complex coordination almost hourly. Photographs monitoring the work in progress are terrifying to the nonengineering eye used to the vessel in her sailing trim and summertime elegance.

All kinds of technical problems were encountered and resolved as the work progressed. The ship's original transverse framing system (explained in Chapter 2) built fully one-third of the ship's strength into the main deck. When large portions of this deck were removed, the ship's shape and strength had to be preserved by installing two powerful rectilinear box girders amidships, in the waist-deck area, to remove any strain on the structure and masts, or compromise to the ship's lines. A technical tragedy of sorts struck when the deck was being renewed. The steel plating of the deck required replacement, but the original teak deck covering it was found to be in relatively good condition. The marvelous Southeast Asian wood had served spendidly but had to be torn up to give access to the aged metal. The original teak planking had been caulked by hand in an era when shipyards took such tasks for granted. But today's people, budgets, and times being what they are, the new deck, though fastened with studs in the old way, had to be grooved by routing and payed with poured sealing compound. Even at that, the more than 25,000 linear feet of new clear teak deck planking, set in mastic, consumed 11,000 studs and 14,000 shipyard staff hours of work. Do not tread softly on *Eagle*'s pristine decks, but do tread appreciatively.

One of the most painful tasks of the great refurbishing effort of the early 1980s was the removal of the fine old teak decks to get at the steel deck plating, here shown in ignominious condition. Fully a third of Eagle's *hull strength resides in the integrity of her main deck. The job had to be done. (U.S. Coast Guard photo by Harry Butt)*

With a draft of seventeen feet, and another deck worth of hold above the waterline, the bilges on *Eagle* are a long way beneath the deck. Roughly 390 tons of pig-iron ballast, in 90-pound loads, one load at a time, had to be drawn from the bottom of the ship up to the deck so that the bilges could be inspected and coated for service into the twenty-first century. This period of the project was not a halcyon time for the shipyard workers.

Though the ship had been distressed in many ways by its use over the years, evidence of its initial high quality kept revealing itself. As had the original teak deck planking, the standing rigging, its cable wire, and fittings stood up to every test that scientific torture could subject it to. After

The port-side bridge wing dominates a portion of Eagle's *torn-up waist deck. The entire original teak deck was removed to get at the rusted steel plating below. Plating and new teak decks were installed from stem to stern, readying* Eagle *for another fifty years of training on the world's oceans. (U.S. Coast Guard photo by L. Drexel)*

half a century, the material continues to perform up to the standards established for it. *Eagle*'s boatswain remarked one day, "It's a darn good thing, too, because these fittings [placing a hand around one of the main lower-shroud "bottle" rigging screws], these right here, aren't made any more!"

On and on the program went. Back in the 1950s the German supply and distribution executives in charge of M.A.N. diesel parts and service inventories would express incredulity when *Eagle* invoices came through from the Coast Guard Academy, ordering a part for "Elmer," the ship's vital main-drive plant. By the 1970s, incredulity had turned to derision, modestly described as levity in the official Coast Guard reports that detail the refurbishing program. Though sporting a new block, supplied by the English postwar (1946) occupiers of the manufactories, the rest of Elmer had been fabricated in 1932, four years before the ship was built. At that time Germany had living, albeit elderly, citizens who had known Herr Daimler, one of the inventors of the diesel internal combustion engine. Here it was 1982, and Elmer still churned away, fallout speed just over nine knots, commanded by a forty-eight-second delay telegraph-response regimen.

Out Elmer came, now gratefully in the possession of *Sagres II* of Portugal, used for parts and so yet giving service, after a billion controlled explosions and the equivalent of a couple of trips to the moon and back in its wake. Its replacement, a Caterpillar D-399, with a 7271 transmission, is a multigenerational descendant of Elmer. It gives the ship 12.3 knots and can be controlled almost instantaneously. Its name is Max, and it has till the late 2120s to equal the performance record and affection won by its precursor.

Some creature comforts were sacrificed in the midst of the rejuvenation

Ventilation conduits are installed during the great refurbishing of the early 1980s. (U.S. Coast Guard photo by Harry Butt)

work. *Eagle*'s officers and seamen who were aboard during that (1981) summer season she sailed with new steel main-deck plates, but without her new teak deck covering, comment on how peculiar the ship seemed that summer. Without all that weight of wood, let alone its security underfoot and its beauty, the vessel handled differently — less positively and pleasantly. And during periods when the habitable areas of the ship were betwixt-and-between, neither the old and familiar nor the new were satisfactory. From the outside at a distance, little seemed to have changed, yet everywhere aboard, things were undergoing revolutionary change. It was becoming altogether a new home for everyone. Today, only a few years later, as service billeting schedules bring to the ship's company inevitable attrition and replacement, soon no one aboard will remember how it used to be.

But all who find themselves aboard these days enjoy incredible privilege, in some ways. The alumni of the ship will remember hammocks, capstan chanteys, and sliding down the stays after working aloft, but today's personnel enjoy advantages in engineering, navigation, boat-drill, ground-tackle, electrical, communication, and ventilation equipment that were considered fantasies enjoyed only on regular cutters a few years ago. Exception for the flag cabin, no part of the ship remains without radical excisions and alterations overhead, and completely revamped underpinnings. Except for the hull itself, *Eagle* is practically a new ship, and any engineer or professional person familiar with modern budgets in labor and materials will be impressed by the relatively modest $9.1 million cost of the

Modern bunks replace the hammocks of old in the main berthing area for cadets. Alumni of the ship say that something is both gained and lost by these comfortable quarters — comfort and privacy added on the one hand, and on the other an historical sense that old-timers feel is missing. Still, home sweet home soon becomes a bunk when one is at sea on arduous duty. (U.S. Coast Guard photo)

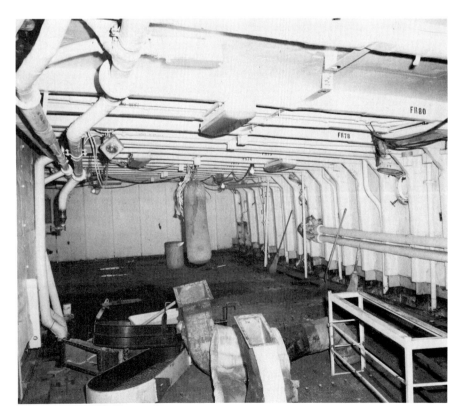

The new berthing area in an early stage during the great refurbishing. Nine new bulkheads were installed in these operations, bringing the ship up to full two-compartment status and modern standards of strength and safety. Notice the relatively light frames along the side of the ship. (U.S. Coast Guard photo)

four-year program, thanks exclusively to the enthusiastic patronage of Congress, and the 230,000 staff hours of restoration work on the project. Technical papers go on for pages listing, describing, and detailing the minutiae of benefits added to the ship. Physically improved, *Eagle* continues her mission. She is now a modern cutter, but the effects that her training platform was commissioned to create are ancient, and they endure.

For nautical enthusiasts, who always like numbers, here are today's ship statistics:

Length, overall	295 feet
Length, at waterline	231 feet
Beam (width)	39.1 feet
Freeboard	9.1 feet
Draft, loaded	17.0 feet
Displacement, loaded	1,816 tons
Ballast, iron pigs	344 tons
Fuel oil	24,215 gallons
Water	56,140 gallons
Fore and main-truck heights	147.3 feet
Mizzen-truck height	132.0 feet
Fore and main-yard lengths	78.8 feet
Sail area	21,350 square feet
Speed, cruising under power	10 knots (12.3 maximum)
Speed, under sail, up to	17 knots
Anchors	3,880 pounds

Eagle's stern and rudderpost. For painting, Eagle's *name and scrollwork are masked. Beauty and maintenance work always converge on a sailing ship.* (U.S. Coast Guard photo by Neil Ruenzel)

Eagle *at Robert E. Derecktor Shipyard dry-dock for routine bottom cleaning and painting. Newport, Rhode Island, winter 1984.* (Courtesy of the artist, Bruce Alderson)

4 Life Aboard *Eagle*

Seamen lay out on the fore royal yard for sail evolutions and pause to look up at the fore topgallant yard, where the photographer has taken us for a bird's-eye view of the ship. (Ed Daniels photo)

Eagle is a small town, though it lacks the typical New England township's gypsy moths in the woodlot and has a government more highly structured than a civilian is used to. The ship's company is housed in distinctive communities and neighborhoods, comprising many classes, groups, and organizations. Though the personality and style of the government change as key officers and personnel come and go, community services must be kept available and operational. On a voyage, as the days at sea pass, the similarity between ship and township remains.

The vessel's primary purpose is training, much of it in practical matters and procedures. This is a company town, with full employment, full civil participation, and no slums. It has no merchants, but it does have butchers, bakers, and electricians. It also has public works, a health department, and churches; and the waist at times becomes a public park for off-duty personnel. The township feeling prevails above all in the ship's society. Despite the chain of command and manifest duties for all those aboard, a genuine sense of community is noticeable. Amid the salutes,

Ship's company and Canadian Coast Guard College graduates relax at the rail, where much shoulder-to-shoulder conference transpires. Shared views pass in constant review as stories are told, opinions are sought, and advice is tendered. The rails receive especially hard workouts when ports of call are approached or left, as here off Portsmouth, New Hampshire, in 1984. (Darcy Davidson photo)

commands, instructions, and steady execution of ship's business, people pass the time of day, talk about life, family, and politics, and indulge in rumors and gossip. Through the times of intense activity, when a hundred cadets scurry about the decks and in the tophamper to tack ship, wisecracks, epithets, and jokes are tossed about. During the languid times, when the sails are drawing and the ship bounds along on course and all is well, here and there around the rail people lean in shoulder-to-shoulder conversations that only they and the seas passing below witness. In odd nooks and corners people read and study. Cadets help one another with their sextants, taking sun sights. Two men who have recently become fathers exchange notes on their wonder at it all as they relieve the watch. A ship's guest at the taffrail watches the storm petrels feed on zooplankton stirred up in *Eagle*'s wake, overhearing the cadet on stern watch report the progress of a fishing trawler on the horizon. A quiet moment in *Eagle* township, and the fascination is endless.

From the bridge deck, the ship's commanding officer (right) surveys the ship's business. (Darcy Davidson photo)

But life here has its differences, too. *Eagle*'s public-address system reaches every corner of the ship. When the vessel is at wharfside and it is announced, "*Eagle* approaching," every person aboard makes a mental note: It's the captain coming. Somehow this event changes the entire ship and life aboard her. "*Eagle* aboard," the speakers announce; things are as they should be....

We are a people very much in touch with our leadership. Our leaders place a definite cast and style on our times and society. Just as we reckon the eras of our lives by presidential terms of office, so ships go through periods designated by the captains in charge of them. It is in the nature of ships that information and command is transmitted almost instantaneously, not just in detail but also with the skipper's style and personality. Nautical literature is filled with tales of good ships and bad, hell ships and happy ones, and nearly always the primary agents in the stories are the sea captains. The way in which U.S. military officers are trained and advance through the ranks of command guarantees technical competence in those who are placed in charge of vessels. With this authority behind him or her, each commanding officer lends to a ship his own way of doing things and often the spirit in which they are done.

Teaching young people is a primary duty for *Eagle*, so special care has always been taken in choosing her captains. *Eagle* is a sailing square-rigger, and so especially able seamanship must be added to excellence in teaching and service record. Her captains have always been the best. This high quality is impressive, coloring not only the ways in which the ship's duties and missions are accomplished, but also the quality of experience for all who are aboard her, including guests.

For a guest aboard, it is uncanny how so many details, demanding so many skills and obligatory styles of execution, can be seen to, accomplished, and reported with so few delays, messings-up, and mistakes as on this training ship, filled with youth and unsureness. No question, it is the skipper, his officers, chief petty officers, and seamen who get things to happen because authority and responsibility are delegated. But really high levels of performance are reached only when trust and implicit expec-

Orders cannot be followed unless they can be heard, and often they cannot be heard unless barked. Experience at sea develops the lungs and voice as well as sea legs and nautical skills. (U.S. Coast Guard photo by Paula Hobson)

tations are also very high. Cadets and young officers who have never ordered or executed a procedure or command in their lives do so with amazing certainty and positiveness on board this ship. A dozen times every day at sea, I watched the skipper smiling while he watched a young man or woman for the first time shout out an order that would change the aspect of 2,000 tons of ship and the lives of 200 people in the service of the United States. Even in the occasional slip-ups, the smile did not disappear. Out would come the supportive arm around the shoulder, a gentle word, and a "Let's try again," or a "Next time it will go better." Off watch and below, the young sailor might castigate or kick him- or herself, or glow with satisfaction. On deck, it is clear that in an era when we all worry about the quality of our republic's teachers, one classroom is eminently secure.

Eagle's wardroom is a headquarters, a living room, a dining room, a meeting room, a classroom, and the ship's foyer; but most of all it is a sanctuary. Although it is plain, even austere in ambience and décor, its multiple functions do not detract from the way in which it is regarded by all those aboard — a place of propriety and authority. A guest of the ship is automatically included in the wardroom's membership, with all its privileges, and now and again its obligations. For this is officer country, and though ranks, billets, duties, and assignments may change, always for officers aboard a vessel of cruising class, this is *their* wardroom. Within minutes of embarking, guests are told by the executive officer that this is *their* wardroom, and that in good faith they should use it as such.

All ships differ, and the brunt of orienting newcomer-guests falls on the officers, who for good reason must regard newcomers as at least potential problems. Along with the physical newness of a ship's environment, where bumped heads, being at the wrong place at the wrong time, and sometimes seasickness can interrupt the normal course of ship's business, greenhorns and visitors can seem to be alien — unknowns in an environment where unknowns cannot long be welcome. Fortunately, officers are also gentlemen and gentlewomen, and so good faith presides in the wardroom, and guests soon figure out their proper role and station.

Observers can soon begin to see into the siblinglike relationship among *Eagle*'s officers. Although all shipboard bucks stop at the captain, by delegation of authority and duty the actual ship's operations and instructional responsibilities move through the officer corps, not just from top to bottom, but also laterally through the ranks of personnel who are each officer's responsibility. Responsibilities aboard the ship are structured less like a pyramid than a tree, with functional stems and twigs coming off the officer branches. On this ship, commissioned to train officers, the implicit assumption among the officers is that they are not just duty-bound to create their own kind, they also instinctively want to do so. Responsibilities among the officers are therefore continuously exchanged. Everyone wants a piece of every ship's action, and this system gives the wardroom the privilege of intense sharing and full understanding. Within a day or two, every officer knows the status, strengths, and weaknesses of every cadet aboard, not only by reputation, but by observation. Thus first-rate tall ships are sailed, and first-rate education is instilled, and the techniques for achieving both all come together in the wardroom.

Under usual circumstances, the wardroom is thoroughly egalitarian, with good humor and all dealings on a first-name basis. When ship's business is in abeyance, the usual conversation is general, though naturally loaded in favor of other ships, other longsplices (as mariners express it), and personal interests. *Eagle*'s officers are more or less at mid-career, and so Coast Guard service gossip is not unknown, and the triumphs and foibles of modern family life are the stuff of both fun and handwringing. It is a very familial place at times. All officers are responsible for mutual peer review and reporting of performance records, but the overall sense is intense mutual interest, sharing, regard, plain loyalty. Some old-school-tie talk is to be expected, but Coast Guard duty implies that all members of the school are continuously cast hither and yon on a thousand different assignments, many of them demanding arduous and dangerous work. Everyone knows everyone else, but opportunities to see one another, to work together in such pleasant and frankly pedagogical circumstances, come rarely in their careers. This privilege of duty aboard *Eagle*, then, fuels a special kind of mutual regard.

At meals it is standard operating procedure to await the executive officer, whose station at the head of the table signals both his authority and his obligation to make announcements, receive debriefings, and occasionally match conversational topics with table mates. Matters are aired at wardroom meals, and especially at dinner. Along with much friendly joshing and banter, serious matters are often broached, and the frankness and candor are striking. Wardroom life is most often interesting and enjoyable, but also intense. Around the clock, the businesses of life and work are mixed aboard *Eagle*.

Ordinarily, the captain takes evening meals in the flag cabin, and if the wardroom is a sanctuary, the flag cabin is an inner sanctum. Its dark wood paneling and elegant furnishings are in the strict tradition of sailing ships, a place where Very Important People can find their proper repose below-decks. The mind's eye depicts the great ship commanders of history brooding, scheming, attempting, and determining that which was to become history in the after cabins of famous vessels. *Eagle*'s flag cabin qualifies in all respects: Fifty years of *Eagle*'s history has happened here, and if Hitler (perhaps) glanced through it on his review tour of the ship at launching, so too seven presidents of the United States, and hundreds of the Coast Guard's finest sea captains, along with admirals, senators, House representatives, and luminaries in every field of civilized endeavor have been welcomed here, and taken their ease.

At sea, flag-cabin guests are posted a week in advance of their expected appearance at dinner. When visiting flag officers are aboard, they are of course included in the venue, but the most special thing about these meals

The flag cabin's saloon (lounge area) — quiet, private, and attractive — is the gathering place for the captain's guests. Authority and gracious ease conspire here each evening before dinner is served. (U.S. Coast Guard photo by Doug Bandos)

is that cadets are almost always included in the guest list. Usually, a ship's officer, a ship's guest, and at least two cadets are invited to join the captain and flag-rank visitors to the formal repast. The mixture of formality, privilege, and historical sensibility can be heartening. On deck, half a gale may be blowing. Up forward, shipboard scandal may be brewing as a dozen cadets realize that the sun may not come out again on the cruise, obviating completion of their navigation requirements. In the wardroom, a junior-grade lieutenant may be receiving just licks over an ill-considered opinion. Meanwhile, in the flag cabin, a couple of cadets and ship's guests are soon relaxed in the congenial presence of the skipper, who need not conjure the clout that is so self-evident. Conversation is gracious, and the food is superb.

Along with the intimations and habits of the ship's society, guests soon learn the daily routing of life aboard, which on a Coast Guard cutter is infused with the traditional disciplines of the military marine through the ages. In bare outline, the day's life seems spare and regimented, but in fact it is rich in variety and detail. Consider this standard *Eagle* Training Cruise Routine of the Day:

Daily	Holiday	At Sea
0630		Reveille
0700–0745	(Note 1)	Breakfast
0755		Muster Dayworkers
		Morning Muster
		Morning Colors
0800		Turn to Ship's Work
0900–0940		Cadet Instruction Period #1
	0930	Catholic Lay Service (Sunday)
0945		Reveille for Midwatch
1000–1015		Coffee Break
1020–1100		Cadet Instruction Period #2
	1015	Protestant Lay Service (Sunday)
1100		Noon Meal for Oncoming Watch
		Secure Ship's Work
1130–1215	(Note 1)	Noon Meal
1150		Noon meal for Offgoing Watch
1200		Test All Alarms and Ship's Whistle
1240	1240	Officers' Call
1245	1245	Quarters Followed by Drills
1415		Turn to Ship's Work
1420–1500		Cadet Instruction Period #3
1500–1630		Study Period
1630		Secure Ship's Work; Sweep Down
1700	1700	Evening Meal for Watch Reliefs

1715–1800	1715–1800	Evening Meal
1730	1730	Evening Meal for
		Watchstanders
		Evening Colors
1900	1900	Check Material Condition Yoke
1945	1945	Evening Reports
2200	2200	Taps — Lights Out

The lower footropes provide a tenuous perch for crew members, who stand by to furl and secure the staysails. With some experience in the rigging, they can indulge in humor, which is irrepressible among sailors. (U.S. Coast Guard photos by Indie Williams [bottom] and Paula Hobson)

Meanwhile, in the Plan of the Day, issued each day by the executive officer, the ship's general routine blossoms into the full, busy daily experience that is *Eagle*'s purpose. It is divided into three parts, though ostensibly listed in numerical order from one onward. Always the first order is to "Carry out the At Sea routine of the day." Then, when appropriate, congratulations are offered to the ship's company for distinguished operations the day before, or as in this one from summer 1985; "Good job by all hands in Boston. More than 5,800 visitors have a little better idea about why we are so proud of our ship." The primary job of this daily document is of course much more specific and mundane, as in the orders reproduced here, selected from a ten-day sail between Boston and the island of Saint Pierre, off the southern coast of Newfoundland. For the most part, these are lectures and demonstrations — the Coast Guard Academy is a college, after all, but some of the daily plan items obviously refer to drills as well.

July 8,		
Second Period:	Rapid radar plotting,	Mess deck
	General engineering	
	and safety,	Mess deck
	Small-boat seamanship	Waist deck
July 9,		
Second Period:	Wearing ship,	Mess deck
	First Aid, Part one	To be announced
Third Period:	Boat lowering,	Waist deck
	Honors & Ceremonies	Mess deck
July 10,		
First Period:	Advanced weather,	Mess deck
	Winches/windlasses	Mess deck
Third Period:	Tacking ship	Mess deck
July 11,		
Third Period:	Ground tackles	
	(anchoring)	Forecastle
July 13,		
Third Period:	Weather observation,	Mess deck
	First Aid, Part two	Mess deck

And so it goes, each of the many sections of cadets receiving their instruction in turn, and then being released for actual practice in what they have

Ship's crew stand by at the man ropes preparing for the order to lower away in a boat drill, at sea, while Eagle *remains underway. Tricky and difficult operations, such drills are part of training for cadets, and of updating for crewmen, who in ordinary service must often launch and manage small craft under dangerous circumstances.* (Photo by the author)

learned, at the appropriate stations, above- or below-decks. The usual rule is for cadets to learn and work in small groups or teams, and so standard lessons are often repeated, as are practice and drill sessions about the ship. Because two classes of cadets are aboard the ship, and each of these is divided into several groups, you can imagine how intricate is the coordinating and managing of these many pedagogical meetings. They must be held and then assessed for their results, making the commissioned and enlisted teaching staff of the ship very busy.

But perhaps the most interesting aspect of the Plan of the Day appears in the simple numbered announcements following each day's ship's work schedule, again here selected from a midsummer week at sea:

1. Parts for the mess-deck popcorn machine are on order. They'll probably be received when *Eagle* returns to New London.
2. Connecticut will be holding a primary election on 10 September and a general election on 5 November. Residents should see the unit voting officer for information or an absentee-ballot request form. VOTE!
3. All hands are reminded not to use the plastic-covered jump ropes. They will damage the deck covering topside.
4. Our present course is taking *Eagle* to the southeast toward the Gulf Stream. The sole purpose of this course is to improve opportunity for celestial navigation. Take advantage of the visibility while you can.
5. Personnel inspection will be held Monday, at quarters. The Superintendent will inspect one of the divisions.
6. As of 0600, 9 July, *Eagle* has observed: 4 twilights, 1 LAN [Local Apparent Noon fix by sextant, wherein latitude is determined by sighting the sun at the apex of its daily arc], 4 navigational days. You should have submitted to your navigational supervisor: 1 celestial fix, 1 celes-

"Oh Lord, my ship's so small...." Every foot we climb aloft makes the ship recede, until at the main truck the deck seems disconnected and remote. Like their physics, perspectives on sailing vessels are remarkable and surprising. Note the class session being conducted on the waist deck. (U.S. Coast Guard photo by Paula Hobson)

The Warrant Boastwain waits for the moment of sunset to check the gyro-compass error. With all of Eagle's *electronic navigation equipment, the ship's exact place on the ocean can be determined. Sunset should occur at a precisely known place on the horizon. To the extent that it sets apparently out of place, the compass is in error, a figure the navigator must know.* (Peter Geisser photo)

tial running fix, 1 gyro error. If you haven't met the requirements, you'd better get to work!

7. Clocks will be advanced at 0800 to +2 0 time zone.
8. Saint Elmo's Fire — light sometimes seen in the rigging at sea caused by static electricity discharge.
9. Yesterday's tacks went very well. The time to regain headway, 6 min. 30 sec., on the second tack, equaled this summer's previous record, set on 18 June. Time to regain a speed of 7 knots was 35 sec. slower than the previous record. Keep working on it. Good job!

10. "Dipping the flag" is a form of salute, or honor, given by a merchant vessel to a passing military vessel. You should always be alert when you pass close aboard a merchant vessel to see if they dip (lower) their ship's flag. If you see a vessel do this, the proper response by the OOD is to lower our national ensign approximately halfway and then immediately two-block it again. As this signal happens the merchant vessel will again raise its national ensign.

> Self-control is the chief element in self-respect, and self-respect is the chief element in courage.
>
> — Thucydides: History of the Peloponnesian Wars c. 404 B.C.

11. If any of you heard the loud boom around 1000 yesterday and don't know what it was, it was the sonic boom caused by the SST Concorde aircraft flying overhead.

12. Morale night is almost here. The First Class Petty Officers promise us the best pizza yet.

13. All cadets are reminded that proper care and stowage of their assigned sextants are cadets' personal responsibility. If your sextant is broken or otherwise unsatisfactory, take it to QMC Oakley or another QM, or LT Baker or LTJG Quedens, for repair. If it cannot be made usable you will turn it in and be assigned to a sextant used by some of your classmates. Treat your sextants carefully, and safeguard them. Convince your classmates that they should not use them without permission, because you are still responsible for their proper stowage.

14. On Wednesday morning 7 July the sailing "Bears" will be racing against the St. Pierre Sailing School. More than 60 cadets, crew, and officers have joined the team. Coach How has recruited top sailors, who he predicts will easily beat any and all opponents. All hands are invited to participate or just join in to cheer the team on. GO BEARS!

15. The ship looked good at yesterday's material inspection. A major improvement has been made in the berthing areas. Let's keep it up.

16. Personnel inspection will be at quarters. The uniform will be tropical blue long with combination caps. Cadets on watch during inspection will be inspected after watch by the CAO.

17. *Eagle* will be under way from anchorage at 0800 Tuesday and moored about an hour later. We will be in a foreign country. Our hosts may not have had much contact with Americans and will form an opinion of our country based on how well we represent it. Respect the customs and be proud to represent our country, the Coast Guard, and *Eagle*.

> Brave admiral, say but one good word; What shall we do when hope is gone? The words leapt like a leaping sound: "Sail on! Sail on! Sail on! Sail on!"
>
> — Joaquin Miller, 1841–1883, Columbus

Aboard a Coast Guard ship, events are sometimes announced electronically, but most often they are piped on the bo's'n's pipe. This ancient instrument, precursor of the public-address system, will never be replaced, just as sextants will not be done away with by electronic navigation equipment. Something in its timbre penetrates to every part of the vessel. A piped message is a heard message. (U.S. Coast Guard photo)

Some things never change, as any sailor will tell you. Years ago Eagle *sailors turned to swabbing the deck in unison, and years from now, they will still be doing it.* (U.S. Coast Guard Academy Archives photo)

Such selections from the ordinary manifests leave out many specialized orders and announcements, but these few give you some idea of how both official and familial aspects are mixed in ship's business, all under the administrative hand of the executive officer, the captain's right-hand officer in charge of the wardroom at all times and the ship generally. Activity aboard ship is continuous, day and night, and so responsibility does not begin or end at any time. Ship's guests will often try to find the best schedule, but this attempt is futile. Reveille and taps are sounded, to be sure, but they have a cursory meaning in a world that sails on the sea. Almost everyone aboard has been up for a full watch during the night — four hours of work as usual.

Not that the piping of reveille does not heighten the pace in the morning; it certainly does. At breakfast the night-watch reports are read, the captain receives the ship's situation and condition summary over his morning coffee, and the Operations, Training, Crew Division, and Cadet Administration Officers confer over their eggs or creamed chipped beef on toast to coordinate their duties during the upcoming training day. Topside, on deck, the low summer sun in the east shimmers through the bracing sea air; already the deck is a scurry of activity — crew and cadets brightly clad

Under full sail, the mainmast presents a wall of canvas. From bottom to top, the square sails are the main course, the lower and upper topsails, the royal, and the topgallant. A cadet in the "tops" works on rigging maintenance. (Peter Geisser photo)

in their oilskins, hosing down and scrubbing the teak decks. Morning aboard a barque.

In Chapter 3 we described *Eagle*'s extraordinary plethora of rigging, fully five miles of cable, wire, and rope, all of which requires continuous care and understanding. Though often as many as 140 cadets are aboard, to do the bidding of the ship's command, generally no more than three or four bo's'n's mates, and nine or ten enlisted seamen billeting aboard, have an

One of Eagle's *seamen does a bit of hard work out on a yard. Repair, maintenance, and replacement of fittings aloft never stop. The difficulty of the chore is described by the adage "One hand for the ship, and one hand for yourself."* (Peter Geisser photo)

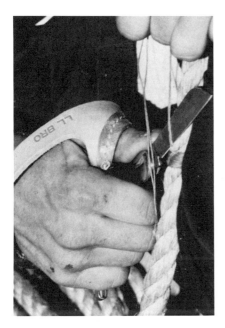 

Bronze, brass, and line require con-stant tending and care. Cadets at a thousand small maintenance duties can be seen all about the ship at all hours. Brass polish and the sail-maker's palm become common ship-board companions. (U.S. Coast Guard Academy photos by James P. Conway)

inner grasp of ship's business. All those ropes and lines, stuck way up there in the sea's corrosive and abusive atmosphere, require constant monitoring, maintenance, and use. Whatever orders are given, whatever conditions prevail, whoever executes the orders under those conditions, things have to be correct when they happen, and both their correctness and details of their use are the responsibility of the sailing master, his boatswains, and his seamen. Anyone who owns a small sailing boat or yacht has had a taste of the sea's toll on spars and rigging. Just multiply that experience a thousand times, and you can understand what sort of ship's husband *Eagle*'s sailing master must be.

Below in the ship, every sort of technical system that any other modern cutter must carry, *Eagle* has also. The maindrive systems, electrical generators, and water and air circulation systems make full-time work for a half-dozen engineering specialists, and their hours are barely enough. Two hundred people are living, day and night, in a 2,000-ton vessel, performing all natural functions, plus those required by their service. A hundred miles of wiring, dozens of miles of piping, valves and meters from one end of the ship to the other — many placed in the peculiar and difficult places that a ship's special shape demands — these are their responsibility.

Above decks and below, intricate systems require assiduous care and, of course, the teaching of them. This is a *training* ship. It is not enough that the warrant officers who are in charge of these systems be competent and correct in their maintenance and use — they must also teach the next generation of Coast Guard mariners all about them. They too must follow the tradition of skipper and commissioned officers; they must be patient and thorough teachers.

One could, without close attention, miss a great deal of the ship's business that hovers about these critical officers. Nearly always someone is aloft in the rigging, seeing to some small but vital detail, but because

In the engine room, the engine's performance is read on dozens of gauges, every one of which is checked and logged at the beginning and the end of every engine-room watch. "Max," the 1000-horsepower main drive plant, dominates the engine room. (U.S. Coast Guard photos by Doug Bandos [top] and Paula Hobson)

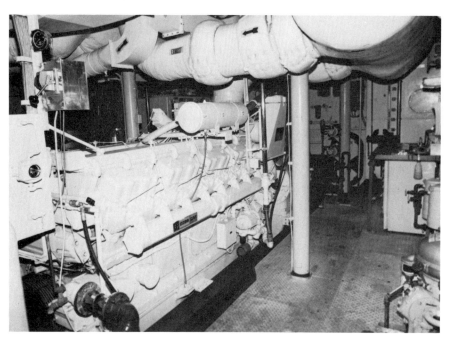

someone is nearly always up there, you soon come to take it for granted. The bo's'n's locker is below-decks forward. As many as a half dozen seamen and cadets will be working there, on a line, a cable, or even woodwork, and the paint locker always has someone in it. . . . Things are always cooking in the boats department, and after a while it becomes easy not to notice, As in a town ashore, people are running the day's business, but you become unmindful. Meanwhile, hundreds of tasks a day, day and night, are accom-

Eagle's main wheel about to be dismantled for repair and adjustment of the main shaft. Meanwhile, the ship's steering is transferred aft to the auxiliary coffin wheel on the poop deck. In the North Atlantic, summer 1985. (U.S. Coast Guard photo by Doug Bandos)

plished on deck and aloft by the sailing master, his chief bo's'n's mates, and seamen.

For anyone in the engineering department, serving aboard a barque can seem almost a tragic error. The romance of sail can appear to drown these fellows in neglect, not for the service and those who know the ship, but certainly for those who cannot see the ship for the rigging.

Upon entering the engine room, your first impression is how *clean* everything is. On a military vessel with military standards and a full complement of officers and cadets whose job it is to see to antiseptic conditions, you could expect exceptional cleanliness, but you could eat off anything in the bowels of *Eagle*. It's not quiet—the main drive, the generators, and the evaporator (which can produce up to 8,000 gallons of fresh water every twenty-four hours) — make the noise of the place spectacular, but it is clean.

A few days out to sea the helmsman notices that the triple steering wheel has an inordinate amount of fore-and-aft play along the shaft. The engineering officer is called to the scene, and it is soon clear that something is wrong with the unit, and that the mechanism must be dismantled for complete diagnosis. Steering is transferred to the after wheel on the poop deck, and the whole main unit is opened up and thoroughly examined. It turns out that during the last overhaul of the mechanism a facing flange was not replaced — not an especially serious problem, just a pesky one of the sort common around large systems. Meanwhile, though, a hundred cadets and crewmen have received a complete briefing on the steering unit. A problem is turned into a classroom exercise, a perfect example of how and why at-sea training is vital to the service. The missing flange? In two hours a perfect bronze flange comes from the ship's machine shop, made right aboard out of stock.

The chief petty officers are the blood-and-bones professionals of the seagoing service. They are the enlisted hands-on officers in the nautical trenches, responsible for the hour-by-hour tasks that must be done on the ship. Along with the bo's'n's mates and enlisted seamen (no more than two dozen of them at any one time aboard *Eagle*), these people are capable of operating the vessel by themselves. Together they are the working core of the ship's company.

These are the people from whom cadets learn most about hands-on operations, and it is a pleasure to watch the pros work with the younger cadets. As in any good school, every instructor has his or her own style. Some have played the crusty old salt for so long that they've become crusty old salts — barking orders, hustling the slow, and springing interrogations on the apparently idle. Others seem more paternal, bringing the neophytes into their confidence as systems are explained and orders executed. And others are out-and-out pedagogical, always lining people up, telling them what they're going to tell them, telling them, and telling them what they told them, ending with a "Got it? Now, let's each of you try it!" All these styles and lessons go on about the ship all day long.

Eagle is a stem-to-stern platform, overtopped by a vast array of rigging, every line of which is entirely in the hands of the crew. We could say that

the same is true of all sorts of modern ships. But managing contemporary non-sail vessels is essentially a matter of electronics: panel-monitoring, dial-glancing, button-pushing, and switch-throwing. To be sure, lookouts are still mandatory, and some elemental seamanship skills are required, but they pale before the moment-to-moment realities of the square-rigger seaman. She is prone to all the exigencies of modern non-sail seamanship, but *Eagle* adds the immediacy of a vast infrastructure: spars, rigging, and sails. Nothing can be left to chance. Every action is either correct or not, and the vicissitudes of sea and atmosphere keep cadets, crew, and officers always alert, continually active, and seldom in emotional doubt as to their station and duty. As with all ships, the paint must be scraped and reapplied, the decks kept well scrubbed, the food prepared and served, the mechanics seen to, the laundry done, and the morale maintained. But up there in the rigging, the larger tale is told. It is there that the first elements of Coast Guard leadership are learned, along with all the other abilities that a modern officer must acquire. The cadet's first experience of the ship is fabulous.

Drills on sailing ships are full of evolutions, a tall ship is an intimidating thing, and the youthful cadet, anticipating his or her shipboard experience, begins growth in the very fearfulness that would stop most elders from considering the adventure. The ship's motive technology and its proportions are grotesque, even in the eyes of experienced small-boat sailors. A thing that has glorious beauty at a distance becomes an overhead visual riot upon actually boarding the ship, and the neophyte mind cannot easily accept its reality and conceive of participation, let alone competence, in the tophamper. It does not beckon the greenhorn recruit. The prospects are scary as hell!

But extraordinarily, cadets quickly find some means to ability, if not

A symphony of sail, each mast a choir, the whole working in concert. (Ed Daniels photos)

Cadets "lay aloft," up the ratlines, into the tops. The old-style sailors' covers (hats) indicate the era prior to 1974. (U.S. Coast Guard photo)

always comfort, in the rigging. Within a few days a cadet who may have taken fifteen minutes to scale the ratlines into the fighting-tops (the first platform on which one can stand) is out on the topgallant and royal yards, high aloft, doing useful work. *Eagle* was purposely designed to be a training vessel, and so it is more forgiving than were the commercial and military ships of former times; nevertheless, the perspective from aloft changes rapidly as you ascend the rigging. From the topmost yards, the ship below looks like a pencil floating on the water. You can see that the mast goes down to the deck, yet it is difficult to accept the connection between your experience aloft and that on deck, where the ship gives you the illusion of vastness. Ships truly are very small on God's great sea, and anyone who goes aloft experiences humility.

For the most part, work aloft consists of freeing the sails from the stops, or gaskets, and furling the sails once they have been brailed-up by the clew lines, leech lines, and buntlines, and, for the staysails, their downhauls (see Chapter 3). Too, maintenance and repair is a constant matter. At least one person is somewhere up in the tophamper nearly all the time. Otherwise, all the necessary drill for handling sails takes place on deck, the product of a thousand years and more of development in sail technology. When you are on duty at a station, with a line or set of lines to control, it is

A foggy day finds a crew member slushing down Eagle's *cable rigging. A mixture of oils and solvent is regularly applied to standing rigging, penetrating to its heart and protecting it from the ravages of the salt-water environment.* (Peter Geisser photo)

difficult to comprehend the splendid orchestration of effort that is required to work a full-rigged square-sail barque.

Observing on the bridge deck, free to move this way and that and in view of those giving orders, you might be standing on the podium next to the ballet's conductor. Perhaps a hundred and fifty people are on deck and in the rigging, standing by at their stations, where about fifteen minutes have gone into preparing their multitudinous lines — mostly freeing the coils from their belaying pins, and faking the lines out over the deck so that they will not tangle or foul when they have to be expeditiously released. When the sailing master calls "Ready about!" a hundred and fifty hearts beat faster. Even those who have sailed all their lives find these ancient orders compelling and exciting. "Fore manned and ready," shouts the foremast captain, followed soon by the main and mizzenmast captains. "Helm's alee!" comes the order, soon followed by "Right [or left] full rudder,

Cadets and enlisted personnel alike stand helm watches, their trick at the wheel; on Eagle *this pleasurable experience goes on at the middle of the bridge deck, the command center and hub of the ship's management at sea.* (Darcy Davidson photo)

sir!" Here we go. . . . The observing officers glance everywhere about the decks, sneaking quick grins at one another.

"Ease the headsail sheets!" "Haul spanker amidships!" As the ship enters the arc of her turn, the mainsails begin to lift, and then comes, "Rise tacks and sheets!" and the mainsails and mizzen staysails are promptly doused. Then, "Mainsail haul!" This, the most famous of orders in square-rigged sailing, sends a chill down your backbone. As the ship goes through the wind, the orders continue: "Shift headsail sheets!" "Ease spanker!" "Ease the helm!" "Let go, and haul!" "Set the main!" We've tacked a square-rigger. Officers and mast captains confer to debrief the drill. A group of off-watch cadets stay in the tophamper watching the boisterous Gulf Stream roll and tumble by. We're doing ten knots.

And sea duty goes on. A painting crew is organized in the waist of the ship, and stanchions are scraped and painted. The after-side of the chart house hosts another crew engaged in more of this sailors' bane. Steel ships do not last fifty years for lack of paint. We are heading north, toward Newfoundland, and our clear weather is not likely to hold out much longer. Cadets who have been remiss in taking and working up their sun sights line the rail with sextants, watches, and notepads. A day later we will hit

"Let go, and haul!" Hands grip and backs get into it during a sail-setting evolution. (U.S. Coast Guard photo by Indie Williams)

Sun and sextant versus sea and weather: twilight navigation sight in progress. (U.S. Coast Guard Academy photo)

the fog and dirty weather, and there will be some contrite cadets.

"For the interest of all aboard, these are porpoises off the port bow." The public-address system routinely announces sea mammals. This time the playful white-sided porpoises grow and grow in number, until they fill the horizon all around the ship. More than a little playful or frisky, some seem actually to go berserk. They leap out of the water in combinations of three, five, eight at a time, in parallel and opposing one another. A half dozen begin to tailwalk, and the ready-boat crew, going through its daily drill, has for an hour a royal escort that Neptune himself might envy. A chief petty officer looks over and asks, "How are you supposed to get any work done around here?" There will be time for that.

A Coast Guard training ship is managed a dozen times over. Plotting, checking, rechecking, cross-checking goes on around the clock. And then it is all done again and again. We are not just running a ship; we are training future professional marine officers. We are not a high-tech navy battlewagon, but we know where we are every minute, nearly as well as any other ship afloat.

Eagle employs all the current standard procedures for navigating ships at sea, and has all the major electronic aids to navigation expected on a modern ship. Between the pilot house and the chart house, the ship's personnel can determine within a score of yards where the ship is on the ocean's surface, and also know what other vessels or obstructions share its part of the ocean, out to a distance of sixty miles. A general principle, indeed a rule, is that everyone aboard a Coast Guard ship is a lookout, and this practice is exactly what you observe on deck. Even during an intense conversation, glances at one another are fleeting. The rest of the time, eyes scan the sea and horizon, and nothing that appears on either goes unremarked.

Even so, official lookouts are posted at the bow, stern, and, often, on the wings of the bridge deck, where pelorus-topped gyrorepeaters stand by to take the bearings of objects or markers sighted by the lookouts. In use, the electronic aids (listed in Chapter 3) are never applied as if they were completely reliable by themselves. Sun sights are always taken when they can be and dead reckoning (using the ship's course and speed to plot position moment by moment) is always kept current, OMNI and SAT-NAV positions are continually acquired and compared, and positions are plotted by radar and pelorus whenever fixed beacons, marks, or land masses are in visual or radio sight. Absolutely every piece of information is taken to be important and must be reported. Even pieces of flotsam on the sea's surface are recorded. As other vessels are raised by sight, or on the radars, a running record of their type (if known), course, and speed is plotted on a rough-log bulletin until they are too far away to cause trouble. It is comforting to see that, on the chart in the starboard pilot house, hatch marks cross the plotted rhumb line of the ship's path every few thousand yards. The frequency is excessive by ordinary standards, but this is how navigation and good seamanship are learned.

A couple of days out, a very large bulk carrier looms on the horizon. She seems at first to be headed well astern of our course, and not much to worry about. Mariners understand, though, the diabolical magnetism that makes ships at sea want to come together, and this ship displays all intentions of intercepting us, and worse. It keeps changing course toward us, getting closer and closer, until the officer of the deck can stand it no more and puts out sparks in the radio shack. A bit of static, and soon a pleasant voice in English, with a thick Swedish accent, says, "Please do not worry about us, my friend. We are just a bunch of sailing nuts having a look. . . ." Swedish bulk carrier crewed by sailing enthusiasts.

On deck at night the ship's society takes on an egalitarian quality. An officer and a group of enlisted men gather around the binnacle and talk about lighthouses and the duty they've served on 44-footers, the Coast Guard's inshore workhorse craft. The electronics technician coddles the 6,000-fathom depth-sounder into responsive perfomance, and talks about art with the navigation officer. He collects books on the French Impressionists. Nearby a group of third-year cadets works at the radar situation simulator, chiding one another's interpretations of the screen's often horrendous announcements. Along the starboard waterway a dozen people watch the moonlight play on the sea's unquiet surface, as they discuss how to quit smoking. A couple of cigarette ends glow brighter, and then are snapped twirling into the ocean. Under full sail, *Eagle* township at sea, at night. . . .

Below, in the wardroom, the talk is about which cadets have still to complete which requirements. In the crew messroom many hands have turned to intensive study, for soon even those who are behind in their assignments will be shuttled off to odd corners or their bunks to make way for the evening film, projected on one side of the mess deck, while a closed-circuit videotape is broadcast on the other side. The ship's professional library calls some, and magazines circulate well. Later the deck will beckon again, before all turn in. That sea is always out there, rolling and

Ship's lookouts make a sighting. Whether it's a boat or ship, a whale, even a bit of floating garbage, lookouts are required to promptly report all sightings to the bridge — not just in the interest of the ship's safety but also to develop the cadets' skill in observation. (U.S. Coast Guard photo by Neil Ruenzel)

Port-side of the pilot house, with collision-prevention control and traffic-monitoring rough-log, center of ship's business. Lookouts report their sightings to this center, and here radar information is evaluated for the ship's safety. Crew members working here have immediate access to the adjacent piloting station, and of course to the Officer of the Deck, who is always nearby. (U.S. Coast Guard photo by Doug Bandos)

tumbling past, a constant spectacle. The ship is turned toward home waters again. Because the sea is a little rough and confused, and the winds are not reliable, the sails are furled and we steam toward Long Island Sound.

Schedules are schedules, and the cadets' thirty-day annual leave is due. The Academy has a routine overhaul in mind for the ship. With the wind's weight out of the sails, *Eagle* is a regular Coast Guard cutter; a bit quick in its rolling motion, perhaps, but in all respects properly at sea, and life aboard goes on as usual.

At breakfast next day, the officer of the deck as usual presents to the captain the current position, situation, and condition report of the ship. This slip of paper includes distance to nearest land and how much fresh water has been consumed in the past twenty-four hours. Halfway through the noon meal, the public-address system announces the pan-shipboard test of all horns and whistles. These half dozen instruments signal everything from sail drill to fire and chemical alerts and fog. They always worked, especially those for fog and sail drill.

A note of triumph appears as we close with land on the homeward approach, calling for a little grandstanding up the Rhode Island shore toward New London on a glorious late summer's day. Good piloting, binoculars, and a running commentary equip the bridge deck's company as we pass through Block Island Sound, around Fisher's Island, and up the Thames River estuary. We will anchor there, in the middle, off the minarets of the Pfizer Company facility. Tomorrow we shall all be ashore,

Looking down from the bowsprit, we see Eagle's figurehead with its perpetual view of coming seas and a bone in the teeth where the cutwater parts the seas in a frothing wave. The bowsprit is a special place to which cadets and other photographers repair for seagoing thoughts and interesting pictures. (U.S. Coast Guard photo by Neil Ruenzel)

Seen from the foremast fighting top, the bowsprit points the way. Views like this reward those who go aloft. (Peter Geisser photo)

pursuing our terrestrial pursuits. This afternoon and evening, *Eagle* tradition rules, for this is the time of the games.

As the ship closes with land on the return voyage, the crew galley turns to pies, for the culmination of the *Eagle* Cruise Olympics is a pie-eating contest. The wind has settled down finally, perfect for olympics. Each class of shipboard society presents a team, and each team does its best in seamanship, the egg-drop, and pie eating. Out of the depths, a delineated scoreboard appears. Decks are cleared for action. First, seamanship is demonstrated by the officers, the chief petty officers, the enlisted crew, the firsties (first-year cadets), and the third-year cadets. Loyalties congeal, and are manifest in slogans and catcalls. We are a ship voluntarily divided.

Each of us receives our assignment. This is the True Test.

"Seamanship" is composed of a relay demonstrating martial skills: connecting and operating a seawater fire pump, in both spray and bail mode; perfectly faking a long length of manila line; tying six standard knots; releasing, donning, and restowing a life jacket; taking a sun shot with sextant; and raising the ship's foretopmaststaysail. This is serious business, the very stuff of the ship's purpose.

The second event is the egg-drop. Aloft on the mainyard each team has a mate with a bucket of eggs, which are dropped one by one to teammates, the largest number of eggs caught, in two levels of intactness, winning the contest. On the deck a large tarpaulin protects the ship. In the heart of man lies the desire to protect eggs.

And then the pipes. It is nip and tuck, but leadership shows its stripes; through fifteen contestants eating three flavors, maturity and commissions show the way. It is not a loaded deck. Cadets can win whenever they

A dramatic backdrop of cloud cover sets off Eagle *as the crew lays aloft to make sea-furl into harbor-furl, transforming loosely controlled sails into the tight and neat furls people are used to seeing when the ship is in port. Here* Eagle *is approaching the Thames River entrance at New London, Connecticut, July 1984. (New London Day photo by Gordon Alexander)*

Coast Guard Academy Superintendent Rear Admiral Edward Nelson Jr. and Captain Ernst Cummings, Eagle's *commanding officer, preside over a portrait of the ship's company during the 1984 sailing season. Halifax, Nova Scotia.* (U.S. Coast Guard photo by Neil Ruenzel)

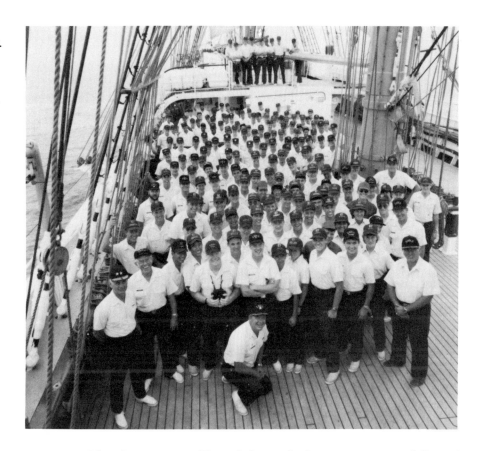

come up with a better team. They do have the best costumes and line of hoopla.

In the evening we have skits, in which anything goes, but their content never goes beyond the rail. The ship is an Alma Mater, a fostering mother. Once you've served aboard her, she forever after is your own ship. So strong is this feeling that even Coast Guardsmen who have never served aboard *Eagle* speak in conversation of "our" ship, and even of "the" barque, in ways they do not when referring to other cutters in the service. *Eagle* is special.

Following another tradition, the captain generally assigns a junior officer who has never conned a vessel into her wharfside berth before to do the job. Usually a breeze is blowing, and even with the sails furled, *Eagle*'s spars and rigging present enormous windage. Too, the river has a strong current. Conning the vessel into a Thames estuary berth is a demanding trick. Days before, a lieutenant commander of the wardroom had marveled at a cadet's expression when one of the officers had executed a complicated harbor maneuver without a pilot or tugboat. "Don't they realize that almost every one of us has had a previous command?" said the lieutenant. Indeed, they have; but have they brought *Eagle* to berth in unsettled weather, in a current?

The captain of *Eagle* has an elegant final instruction for all his officers of the deck who are about to take charge in difficult circumstances: "We don't want to become a restaurant!"

Why an *Eagle?* 5

In official Coast Guard parlance, *Eagle* is often referred to as a training platform, an apt expression, for the Academy has very specific, ancient, and proven goals and on-board objectives in sponsoring *Eagle*. The job is much more than training young people in professional military and nautical skills and instilling features and habits that make up strong and good personal character, although this mission is important too. Underpinning the training are instincts that have shaped and remain vital to our national character, and that came out of our maritime heritage.

Until recently, the advantages of transporting resources, goods, and people by water, instead of overland, were clear to economically active people. Boats evolved into well-developed and efficient ships soon after marine resources were discovered, and so too the knowledge and skills to exploit the sea. The primitive quickly became sophisticated.

Most roads, in most places, throughout most of history, have been poor going. Even in times of peace, under civil-minded leaders, overland transport has always been difficult, a pattern that changed only with railroads in the nineteenth century and our present federal Interstate Highway System. Even the colonial turnpikes, post roads, stage roads, and well-used interurban thoroughfares would not be tolerated by contemporary travelers. These routes were, and in many parts of the world remain, rutted, washed-out, pothole- and bandit-infested travesties.

For military, transport, and trade considerations, then, sea routes were usually preferred. These were limited only by the quantity and quality of ships, and the will and skill of mariners to sail them.

Technological developments came swiftly in design and construction of ships, chandlery, fitting out, and supply. The seaworthy ships' hulls developed by northern European shipwrights, descendants of the Vikings and other Germanic peoples, were combined with the sail-and-rigging technology devised by Mediterranean boatswains from the time of Christ.

Greater size soon was demanded, requiring technological advances just when the early glimmers of the Industrial Revolution yielded the coking of coal, and so there was a rapid increase in the quantity and quality of iron

Meeting personal challenges lies at the core of the Coast Guard Academy's curriculum. A cadet atop one of Eagle's yards shows a proud expression of this. (Darcy Davidson photo)

castings and forgings in steel. Ships and their fittings became better and more numerous, and guns larger and more reliable. Nations that meant to remain sovereign and viable had to make more, bigger, and better ships, with more and larger guns, and with more and better sailors to man them. Where Christopher Columbus faced the possibility of a mid-Atlantic mutiny in 1492, on board ships of a relatively small transitional type, Francis Drake, a hundred years later, had nearly to force a return home to England from Pacific waters. Seamen who once chose long overland trips to avoid passages around major capes, or across large stretches of sea, in one century compulsively sought to gain by sea voyages all they could get of riches and glory. Better and larger ships created stouter hearts and mariners with far more skill.

The Great Age of Sail followed, and though we rebelled against Great Britain, our maritime legacy is essentially British, drawn from a navy that monitored a global empire. Our sense and sensibilities about freedom are directly connected to ships, the sea, and our European maritime roots. They are connected to sailing ships, of which *Eagle* is a perfect example. Our freedoms may, today, be maintained under the power of internal combustion, diesel-electric, and nuclear energies. But they were first felt, created, and won under sail.

Skills

And when we think of sailing, we come to the teaching of skills amid an officers' corps. From the thousands of colonial seamen and fishermen, the Pilgrim Fathers, the men of the *Constitution* in her glory, the mariners of the fast clippers and profitable down-easters, our legacy, besides a romantic history indulged by sailing-ship buffs, is their sense of ability, competence, self-assuredness, and adaptability under duress.

Implicit in *Eagle*'s existence and duties is a profound educational philosophy. First, almost everything that happens on a sailing ship is deliberate and real, uncluttered by subtlety, second-guessing, innuendo, or guile. Second, everything one does on a sailing vessel has immediate consequences, an educational environment that is rare, these days. In this setting, young people can experience real self-evident success or failure in performing tasks.

As men and women go to work, to negotiate their positions in the world, they find that in many critical roles performance of duty is not amenable to doubt and discussion. One does not want one's heart surgeon to have negotiated an A minus in medical-school anatomy class. The modern world is complex, subtle, and difficult, but some things remain crucial and absolute, among them, the performance of Coast Guard personnel. The seriousness of Coast Guard Academy cadets brings focus to their training very quickly. The eighteen- or nineteen-year-old who decides to serve the nation in the Coast Guard must have serious intentions, but a square-rigger's tophamper is a severe and radical place in which to express seriousness. Its onerousness is enhanced by its constant repetition and by ancillary duties on deck and below. President John F. Kennedy, soon after a 1962 visit aboard *Eagle*, said: "I'm not sure that there are many other Americans that could climb that rigging and unfurl those sails in good times and in bad times. I think the American people have too long been unaware of the high quality and high caliber of the cadets of the Coast Guard." It is common for a cadet to be continuously, publicly visible to the ship's company, from first watch to last, without letup. Over days, weeks, and months, year to year, little in one's character is missed, and a cadet is assessed not only for performance of duty, but also for flexibility and adaptability under adverse circumstances. The *Eagle*'s elegant educational philosophy is: identify

President John F. Kennedy presides at the lectern on the waist deck of Eagle *at the Washington Navy Yard, August 1962. Among our nation's leaders, Kennedy perhaps understood best the seamanship that a sailing barque such as* Eagle *can teach.* (U.S. Coast Guard photo)

native talent, train it, and then *observe* that the cadet decidedly knows that he or she commands a competent presence. Once this state is reached, there is very little that the officer cannot afterward learn or be trusted with.

Academy Missions for *Eagle*

The training goals that stem from Coast Guard policy change slightly from year to year, and more extensively from era to era, but current official statements about what *Eagle* is meant to accomplish are typical. Specifically, the ship's mission is to:

Prepare cadets for their initial tour afloat by:

1. exposing them to all aspects of shipboard life, including shipboard traditions, practices, and etiquette;
2. providing them opportunities to apply and develop professional seagoing skills beyond their classroom training;
3. giving them shipboard duties and responsibilities (commensurate with their training level) ranging from entry-level enlisted to division officer;
4. allowing them to exercise and develop supervisory and leadership skills in a realistic yet controlled operational setting;
5. instilling appreciation for the professionalism, teamwork, and camaraderie common to all successful operational units; and
6. encouraging respect and liking for the sea and its lore.

In accomplishing this mission *Eagle* shall emphasize maximum "hands-on" cadet participation in every phase of shipboard operation and life. In general, assigned officers and petty officers will be safety observers, intervening in shipboard operation only for instruction or safety purposes. *Eagle* will train Third Class cadets (Fourth Class during short cruises) in the duties of petty officers and nonrated personnel while assigning upper class cadets the responsibilities of senior petty officers and junior officers.*

In such terse language resides much experience and duty. These Academy goals in commissioning *Eagle* are thoughtfully sought in specific training objectives, organized by class over four years, in four areas of performance expectations: General, Operations, Deck, and Engineering/ Damage Control. Because the first-class cadets (equivalent to seniors in a liberal-arts college) are the most advanced, less than a year away from earning commissions as Coast Guard officers, we'll use here the objectives delineated for them.

Some general characteristics, abilities, and sensibilities are specified that the senior cadets have to demonstrate in their shipboard deportment. These are more than a matter of style, but some of that is implied, for leadership always requires more than plain competence, which often must *demand* respect. Confident style *commands* respect, an important difference. These men and women in their final cadet year must show respect for the vicissitudes of weather as well as for a seagoing vessel's vulnerability to the forces of sea and wind. Their safety consciousness must be demonstrated in their way of relating to the ship and to one another — not just in

*From Superintendent's unclassified in-house Academy document, *"ANNEX S TO COMLANTAREA OPORD 4-(85) CADET TRAINING."*

theory, but in moment-to-moment practice. By the fourth year, a firstie's use of the language should have changed, to incorporate fully the bounty of marine, nautical, and technical terminology that their careers will require. Coast Guard cadets lose forever their "kitchens" and "bathrooms" to "galleys" and "heads." Their habits as shipmates and fellow senior cadet officers must include a visible inclination to continuous, candid self-assessment, to realize their own personal strengths and weaknesses and not to cover up any of these. They will spend years filling out performance reports on other people, so that honest self-regard matters. Furthermore, in a world of rapidly advancing technology, their use of professional publications in fulfilling their "Watch Qualifications" (the highly detailed check-off of blue books of cadet life) must be demonstrated. Finally, as senior officers daily watch and interact with the first-class cadets, they look for those with special ability to work into teams, on the one hand, and the talent necessary to effectively supervise others, on the other. When these two responsibilities inevitably conflict, the cadet's way of resolving the difficulties is also closely observed. The first-class cadet must be seen to act like the junior officer he or she will soon become. Captain Bill Earle, former commanding officer of *Eagle* and still active in the interests of the Academy, quotes a first-class female cadet in a recent issue of the Coast Guard's Academy Alumni Association's magazine, *The Bulletin:*

> "As a third classman I was fascinated by *Eagle* but fearful of working aloft," said Sarah. "I did it, but I didn't like it. When first-class year came along I decided to see if I could conquer that fear. I volunteered to go back to *Eagle.*"
> "Did you get over your fear?" I asked. "I sure did," she replied. "Working aloft with underclassmen, I forgot all about it. They were looking to me. I couldn't be hesitant or fearful when I was supposed to be leading them."
> "Did working with male underclassmen cause you any problem?" I asked.
> "I didn't let any develop," she said with a grin. "I figured if I knew my job and did it, being first class was enough. It was."

Reflecting on his years aboard *Eagle* as a cadet, and then as an officer aboard in various capacities, including executive officer, Captain James Heydenreich said almost sternly, "There is nothing that can touch that ship [*Eagle*] for giving cadets the real thing about being at sea, and making sea duty its responsibilities really part of you. Being a cadet, and being in charge, are very different things, but they are definitely connected."

In an address at the change-of-command ceremonies for *Eagle* in 1983, Rear Admiral Edward Nelson, Jr., superintendent of the Academy, had this to say about *Eagle*'s role in cadet training:

> *Eagle* offers a unique experience. Cadets gain a special appreciation for the sea when they rely on the force of the winds and currents for their progress. *Eagle* enables many young men and women to put in practice the theoretical knowledge they have learned and to test it without suffering terrible consequences for failure. At the same time, however, *Eagle* presents challenges not met on other ships that do pose serious consequences for failure. Working

aloft is a challenge, eagerly sought by some, met and equalled by all who sail *Eagle*.

She is a perfect testing laboratory. Cadets learn about themselves on *Eagle* and whether they have some of the qualities the Coast Guard demands of its officers: bold courage to overcome personal anxiety to do a job which must be done; endurance to continue despite cold, rain and not quite enough sleep; tolerance to accept close quarters and little privacy.

They learn that this ship cannot be sailed without the efforts of all, but that with coordinated teamwork she is an efficient and graceful thing of beauty.

The mid-1970s brought changes to the Coast Guard Service, to the Academy, and to Eagle. *Here some of the first female cadets are pictured on the foc'sle deck during the summer cruise to Hamburg, Germany, in 1977.* (U.S. Coast Guard photo)

Eagle cadets can claim bragging rights on a title few can gain — a square-rigger sailor. Further, that all landlubbers, sand peeps, sailors of mechanical vessels, sand crabs and other derelicts of the seas and shores must acknowledge and pay homage to a true sailor.

Objectives in the other three training areas are more precisely defined. Under Operations, each objective begins with an action verb: demonstrate, operate, communicate, assess, perform, supervise, and so on. Cadets must *show* that they have a working knowledge of all the duties and responsibilities of an officer of the deck, both in port and under way. They demonstrate this knowledge by actually being in charge of the ship, with senior officers of the vessel self-consciously at other tasks, monitoring activities and the cadets' performance from afar, though not too far. This ability must exceed mere line-item knowledge. Scope and depth of understanding must be evident, as well. By their fourth year, these young men and women have stood many watches at every station by which they are surrounded on the bridge. They know from experience the problems each of their shipmates has at a station, and so, when they are in charge of it all, their ability to coordinate the various roles and operations is scrutinized.

These leadership tasks in no way obviate their further training in the operation of ship's facilities. If they have stood a score or more watches at every piece of equipment already, they do so again, each time adding a bit more accuracy, speed, and subtlety in control and interpretation of gear and results. Competence at navigation consoles, ship's controls, and communications devices is never complete. These symptoms of learning vitality must be shown during all drills, whether in practice or genuine urgency. Look briefly at this list of topics covered in the *Eagle* summer-cruise program, as taken from the ship's officer's Academy document on the subject:

TOPIC

1. Shipboard Safety & Escape routes
2. Firefighting & Collision
3. Rules of the Road (Vessel not under way)
4. Rules of the Road
5. Boat Lowering & Raising
6. Required Lights System
7. DC PUMPS (should give short review of use of pumps, then allow each cadet to set up and operate them)
8. Review of Loran/RDF/Fathometer/Radar (should stress use of gear aboard individual unit and give cadets a chance to use gear under supervision)
9. Shoring (should give short review of theory, then allow team of cadets to actually shore a bulkhead)
10. Deck Maintenance supervision (lesson should stress detail of preparation for painting, use of paints, lubricants, etc., on a First LT/CPO level)
11. Main propulsion system

12. Vessel auxiliaries
13. Vessel Boiler/evaporation systems (Lessons 16–18 should stress the practical rather than the theoretical aspect of the engineering spaces, explanation of various gauges & meters, & the significance & operation of gear)
14. Weather — General Theory
15. Radiotelephone Review (should be a very quick review of general procedure; should heavily stress communication security & use of authentication systems)
16. Procedures for anchoring and mooring alongside (OOD)
17. Signaling Review (should stress details of signaling such as time, distances, bearings, & unusual signals)
18. Review of Sight Reduction, Azimuths, & Amplitudes (should stress techniques of using sextant, bearing circles, stopwatches, starfinders, etc., & a quick review of computations)
19. Towing supervisor procedures (should stress items that the supervisor should look out for; demonstrate layout of ship's gear; quick review of general procedures)
20. Internal Ship Security Theory
21. CG Boarding Officer's duties
22. Duties of Auxiliary/ Electrical Officer
23. Visual Signaling Review (should stress procedures & use, location of ship's gear, & message format)
24. Highline supervisory procedures (stress items that the supervisor should look out for; demonstrate ship's highline rigging; quick review of general procedures)
25. Advance Weather (stress interpretation of weather maps/ messages, prediction of weather from local changes in clouds, winds, barometer, etc.)
26. Conducting the Search (should stress the bridge & lookout procedures as well as CIC activities)
27. Search communications
28. Duties of Communications Officer
29. Duties of Exchange Officer & Wardroom Mess Treasurer

Every one of these items of study and practice, expressed succinctly and simply in the schedule, entails hours of learning and review, several sessions of hands-on work, and for the first-class cadet often at least some responsibility for passing the rudiments of these topics on to third- or fourth-class cadets.

Like most cutters in the Coast Guard service, *Eagle* has aboard a most

Under the ship's doctor's supervision, a Coast Guard corpsman practices eye, ear, nose, and throat examination. Because the service often works in small units, corpsmen must be well trained to meet any emergency until full medical service can be reached. (U.S. Coast Guard photo by Doug Bandos)

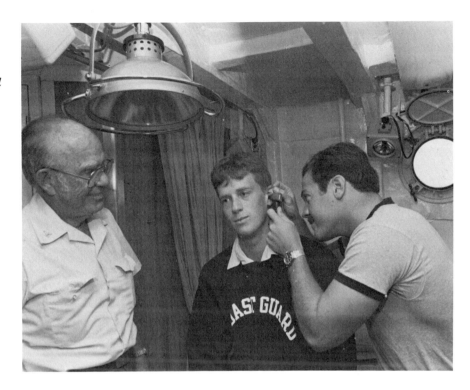

unhappy fellow named Oscar, a life-size dummy, in various states of repair and undress, which (or who) is at odd and unannounced moments thrown overboard, quickly initiating a man-overboard drill. All cadets aboard have read about man-overboard procedures in their seamanship manuals several times, attended lectures on these procedures, and observed them in training films, dockside practice drills at the Academy, and as young cadets on earlier *Eagle* cruises. Oscar's misfortune is much more immediate to the first-class cadets. He is a drowning person in the ocean and the cadets are in the boats. The boat is carefully lowered, the engine is started as soon as the boat strikes the water, the sea painter (bow line) is released, and the boat is off over the sea to get Oscar while the watch on deck never once takes it eyes off the stricken dummy. The drill ends when Oscar is back aboard the ship, often starting a first-aid practice session. All is done while the vessel is sailing under way, but the senior cadets are watched *very* closely. The younger cadets are learning the ropes, but the firsties are expected to be right on top of the procedures, and to execute them with alacrity, even with ease and grace. Lifesaving and response to disaster will be a continuous career duty, and in this, the eleventh hour of their formal training, a penchant for it must be shown.

The same demanding standards apply to their general seamanship. No longer are their demonstrated skills in navigation, piloting, collision-avoidance, procedures for common shipboard "evolutions," sail stations, and boat drills merely items to be checked off. They must be seen to be at least at the threshold of comfort in these activities, and manifestly developing leadership in them, with hands on the conduct of the ship. Even in a complex situation, say with troublesome weather and lots of marine traffic

"Lay aloft and furl!" Following this command, cadets lay out along the yard, standing on the footropes, and work together to gather in the sail, which has been partially furled from the deck via the leech lines, bunt lines, and clew lines. The sail yard is graceful and delicate from a distance; the crew members' perspective gives its true dimensions. Each yard weighs several thousand pounds. (U.S Coast Guard photo by Neil Ruenzel)

in a roadstead or estuary, senior officers on the bridge look for right answers and correct analysis from their senior cadets, so that a simple nod of the head gets orders in response going out to the operations stations promptly, clearly, in proper order, and smoothly. And, when the time comes to report, facility with paperwork, too, must be demonstrated. Senior cadets can look forward to full participation in a bureaucratic age, and their required Port Briefings to the commanding officer will be examined for all the qualities that a career often spent at typewriter and computer console will demand, including correct use of perhaps half a thousand militarily prescribed acronyms.

At anchor, cadets practice at sail drill. (U.S. Coast Guard photo by Indie Williams)

Training objectives focus on the Deck, and Engineering/Damage-Control also goes beyond practice, into the realm of supervision. Final-year cadets commonly find themselves aboard *Eagle* at the pinrails in charge of ten or a dozen junior shipmates or working through others at the masts. Similarly, when routine deck evolutions, cargo handling, anchoring procedures, or anything having to do with the boats is at hand, up to two dozen ship's personnel will be at his or her beck, call, and complete responsibility. To be sure, enlisted seamen and petty officers are often about and involved, but ordinarily the cadet placed in charge is given full scope to either succeed or fall short. Those with three seasons aboard the ship under their belts usually have enough experience that they do not require intervention by those who are already professionals. When it comes time to hand, reef, and steer, or manage a boat alongside the ship, the ship's professional staff again stands aside to watch, and if the chief warrant bo's'n occasionally has his heart in his throat, so much the worse for the boatswain. The senior cadet is trying his or her wings, for good or ill, and heart-in-throat symptoms mean that lots of effort has been put into conjuring the good performance.

One day, at sea, after a particularly active series of sail evolutions (tacking ship through the wind), Captain Ernst Cummings and Rear Admiral Edward Nelson are conferring through broad smiles on the bridge. Asked about their obvious pleasure, they recall, from their own times at the mast, a foible that had nearly happened moments before when a line was being heaved through a purchase (a block and tackle) without releasing another line across the ship, endangering the main yard by subjecting it to severe bending, a serious mistake. When asked, then why

Four-stripers confer, moving and shaking the course of ships and cadets. In the Gulf of St. Lawrence in June 1984, Captain Joseph E. Vorbach (left), Coast Guard Academy commandant of cadets, shares a thought with Captain Ernst Cummings, commanding officer of Eagle *at time of writing.* (U.S. Coast Guard photo by Doug Bandos)

the levity, the captain said, "Hey, this is why we're here!"

The same procedure goes on down in the engine room, and throughout *Eagle*'s complex innards. Three years of classroom and laboratory work, dealing directly with the ship's equipment under others, often finds the senior cadet with weighty responsibilities here, too. As classmates act as officers of the deck above, so too fellowship applies to cadet engineering officers of the watch below. Beyond knowing about the main propulsion plant and the many auxiliary units, cadets must understand how these complicated units depend upon one another in a vast network of connections, energy conversions, and transfers. Relatively small events at one place in the system can have consequences and ramifications at possibly remote places — even pandemic results. The internal medicine of seagoing vessels is every bit as complicated and vital as its seamanship and navigation, and the same high expectations apply below-decks.

Broader understanding is expected of a firstie here, too. Training and evaluation of the cadet in the engine room is like that in the rigging and tophamper. Just as cadets in the tophamper must understand why centuries of nautical experience under sail dictate the way in which lines and ropes run as they do, so the engineering program directs its charges to understand the *design* behind marine mechanics and electronics. Because of the special exigencies of shipboard energy systems, knowing the ways of plant technologies is not enough, for most marine disasters these days are caused by failures in the mechanical devices and operations of vessels, many of them deriving from problems in conception, design, specification, and installation of the systems. Because the average Coast Guard cadet can look forward to perhaps hundreds of marine emergencies stemming from mechanical or electrical failure in boats and vessels at sea, *Eagle*'s training program strongly emphasizes engineering systems design. People who will board a thousand watercraft as inspectors in the public interest should have models for comparison, and *Eagle* is one of them.

Enthusiasm for mechanics and design is also encouraged. When *Eagle*'s water maker, a high-capacity seawater evaporator, broke down, it appeared that the ship would have to go on permanent water rations into the following season. Feeling challenged, several of the ship's crew one day latched on to the problem and devoted themselves to it without let-up for two full days and the intervening night. It should have been exhausting, but instead the crew found satisfaction beyond fulfilling their duty, or working up to the ship's ordinarily high standards. Not only was the broken part (shaft on the saline water recirculator) repaired, but the whole unit was thoroughly gone over, doubling its former output. Asked about this sort of thing, the Warrant Engineering Officer, smirking, said, "Yes, sometimes you'd think these guys like to see things break, just so that they can get their hands on them." Splendid learning environments are created by such people. No one can guarantee that such enthusiasm will rub off on cadets, but it does, as you can see when first-class cadets, off watch, take the long fiddley companionway down to the engine room, to look once again at a unit that has become theirs. A skill is transformed into something much greater.

<table>
<tr><td>

___ O   12. Discuss the following with regard to proper relief of the radar operator watch.

    a. Status of radar
    b. Power output/antenna
    c. Contacts, expected landfall
    d. Last tuning

___ O   13. Discuss the following with regard to proper relief of the surface summary plotter:

    a. Logs
    b. Info on bridge
    c. Labeling of plots

___ O   14. Discuss the effects of the following with regard to maneuvering board solutions:

    a. Radar repeater calibration
    b. Radar operator
    c. Scale selection
    d. Time (period of plot marks, accuracy of period)

___ O   15. Discuss the advantages and disadvantages of:

    a. Ship's service telephones
    b. Multichannel circuits (21 MC)
    c. Sound-powered phone circuits

17
</td><td>

___ O   16. Discuss the type of information generally passed on:

    a. Ship's service telephones
    b. Multichannel circuits (21 MC)
    c. Sound-powered phone circuits

___ D   17. Demonstrate use of the 21 MC including proper phraseology and manual override of a circuit.

___ W   18. For each component listed below, explain what the component does and diagram the location of the component within CIC.

    a. Gyrocompass repeater
    b. Radar repeaters
    c. Radio telephones
    d. Remote radio telephones
    e. Anemometer repeater
    f. Sound-powered phone jack boxes and the circuit
    g. MC unit
    h. Status boards
    i. Doppler unit

___ O/D   19. Point out the location of the following radar controls and explain/demonstrate what each does.

    a. Contrast control
    b. Video gain control

18
</td></tr>
</table>

USCGC EAGLE (WIX 327)

1/C CADET WATCH QUALIFICATION STANDARDS

SUMMER 1985

Character

First-class cadets are formally responsible for evaluating the performance of third-class cadets while aboard *Eagle*. Much of this assessment naturally has to do with specific skills of the type we have discussed. Along with performance skills, adaptiveness receives strong emphasis. After a cadet has met all formal professional training requirements, evaluation remains primarily focused on adaptive qualities, so much that a person's career can be deeply affected. The official Academy directive on evaluating and reporting cadets' adaptive skills lists qualities that are to be assessed:

The bane and strength of the cadet program aboard Eagle: *Cadet Qualification Standards. Every cadet has a copy, for his or her class and season aboard, and every qualification must be checked off and initialed by season's end. They demand comprehensive and high nautical standards.* (U.S. Coast Guard Academy publication)

Personal hygiene; cleanliness	Judgment
Communication skills	Accountability
Coordination	Sensitivity
Self-image or confidence	Personal interaction with
Ability to adjust to new situations and to work under stress	peer groups, seniors or juniors Loyalty Attitude
Force and control	Sobriety
Acceptance of responsibility	Enthusiasm
Dependability	

In civilian life, most of us, most of the time, are commonly judging our fellows, just as we are judged. But this evaluation is usually an informal and slippery thing, subject to occasional outbursts perhaps, but it is done in passing. In this extraordinary organization, on this extraordinary ship, all their professional lives officers of the United States Coast Guard ply

Life on Eagle *is not all spent aloft or on deck. Hours of study below-decks are required to pass all the qualifications specified for a cruise.* (Peter Geisser photo)

their work under official scrutiny, and part of their work is to scrutinize others. This responsibility may seem harsh, but in fact it simply formalizes a duty that any organization requiring precise and reliable performance expects, even if no pieces of paper outline its details. It begins at the beginning for cadets, on *Eagle* and throughout the Academy's training program.

By the fourth year, the Academy has usually winnowed the unfit. After four years the Coast Guard cadet has sailed from greenhorn fourth class to a first-class Officer of the Watch, in all capacities from seaman through mate, engineer, boatswain, navigator, communicator, coxswain weather officer, mast captain, cook and bottle-washer, boat-steerer — almost every role that shipboard training demands. Each has performed these duties not simply as a student, but as the person in full cognizance of and responsibility for the duty. It is as if a small town turned over all its critical functions to its most talented youths; and the evidence grows that this decision may not be a bad idea!

The commissioned officers of *Eagle* are assigned aboard the ship not only for their generally recognized competence and ability, they are also there as a reward for duty well done elsewhere in the service. Officer duty aboard *Eagle* is an unmitigated privilege and the outspoken goal of many in the Coast Guard officer corps who have not (yet) served aboard her. But the public gives perhaps too much attention to the commissioned afterguard (officers) of a training vessel such as *Eagle*. True, they are among the best the service has, and for this reason they have the good sense to stay in background as much as possible. After all, future officers will perform most of their service duties over enlisted personnel, so that much of the actual training and leader interchange aboard the ship is between cadets and professional enlisted noncommissioned officers. These enlisted professionals are also aboard because of extraordinary merit. By sheer force of personality, sometimes verging on magnetism, the chiefs infuse in the cadets under them not only the information they need to discharge their duties, but also the enthusiasm and character to do so. They do this job in the old-fashioned way — by example. Often it is the chiefs, and not senior cadets, who give direct orders and instruction to the cadet corps, and it is a matter of principle that a chief will not order anyone else to do what he or she is not able and willing himself, or herself, to perform. Life aboard *Eagle* is a constant sharing of duties and responsibilities; and if one person is a bit better at a skill, under some conditions, his or her strength is duly remarked, and measures are taken to see to it that these penchants are not unfairly exploited, but rather are passed on and fully shared. All the while, the noncommissioned pros are encouraging, instructing, sometimes needling and teasing, most of the time providing wit and wisdom in the work of creating an ever-better ship, ever-better commissioned officers.

Few efforts in a Coast Guard officer's career do not involve intensive sharing of responsibility under conditions in which each individual must perform as expected, and expect in kind that corps and crewmates will do the same, beyond any doubt. If expecting that twenty-five or thirty fellow cadets will work in concert, exactly as expected, in a difficult maneuver, seems rather a lot to count on, then so be it. At first a lot of mistakes, foul-ups, and confused procedures will come up, but *Eagle* is a forgiving vessel, designed from her inception to tolerate the foibles of tyros, within reason. Meanwhile, the practiced cadet trainee does in fact perform as expected, doing reliably that which is ordered. Launching a lifeboat in breaking seas, manning a helicopter in violent air currents over a burning ship, approaching a smuggling boat known to be armed, and the hundreds of often tedious chores daily performed by the service demand character as well as skill.

Military Readiness: *Eagle*'s Direct Service to the U.S.C.G.

Some words must be said about *Eagle*'s role as a cutter in our nation's service, both a historical and military perspective. In many ways, our American Revolution continues. As our democracy matures and the world becomes ever smaller because of modern transportation and communication technologies, the difficulties and responsibilities of a free people increase. No longer do vast oceans protect us from the realities and consequences of events half a planet away. We can even watch far-off events as they occur. We no longer have the wait-and-see luxury of letting history elsewhere simply take its course.

Our world is a precipitous one, and the media clichés are quite correct. A city becomes a tinder box, situations are explosive, terrorists are rampant, and so on. And when our political leaders perceive that our national interests are somehow involved in these volatile events, they have very little time in which to properly respond. When such a response calls for a military presence, whether militarily active or simply *there* in a monitoring capacity, the military must be able to move with speed, precision, efficiency, and prudence. These often contradictory demands require special features in an officer corps. It may seem a little out of place to speak of military requirements in a book about a peacetime service and its sail-training vessel, but such perceptions are incorrect. For the Coast Guard and its ship are directly implicated in several ways, and for several reasons.

The Coast Guard has always been a fully integrated component of the nation's defense. It was our first navy; its men and ships were actively engaged in both support and combat in all of our nation's conflicts. In spite of the misconception of many citizens, including personnel in other services, the Coast Guard is in all respects an armed service. The Coast Guard is different in that it is always engaged in active combat duty as a service. In effect, every minute of every day is spent in combat, not simply standing by to meet emergencies, but actually meeting them, minute by minute. Whereas all the other services have their drills, scrambles, high-condition-status operations, and war games, which are facsimiles of real situations, the United States Coast Guard is on duty, in fact, every minute: breaking ice and keeping station in remote arctic environments; saving the lives of

Eagle's *magnificient parade colors, the United States ensign. Technically, this one is oversize (all Coast Guard cutters must fly prescribed sizes). But Eagle's special proportions and square-rigger tradition call for a larger flag, here set off by cadets in the mizzen rigging during a July 1984 visit to Portsmouth, New Hampshire.* (Darcy Davidson photo)

distressed mariners under terrible marine conditions; approaching and arresting armed crews of drug-carrying and other contraband vessels and planes; monitoring and inspecting foreign fishing fleets (which are often of the Eastern Bloc, and not entirely what they seem); and otherwise daily performing duties in active and real-time situations. The Coast Guard is engaged in combat, sometimes under combat conditions, against weather and climate, human weakness and stupidity, misfortune and tragedy, criminal cynicism, and active enemies of the United States.

Officers of this service, then, are not only asked to understand their *potential* role, under *potential* circumstances. From the beginning, they are assigned to perform their tasks under actual combat circumstances from the moment they receive their commissions — indeed, before then, on *Eagle,* and this reality deserves elaboration.

Although *Eagle* is essentially a ship of peace and educational provender — no gun sits on her foredeck, and it is not her ostensible duty to make arrests — she is armed with small ordnance, and is authorized to perform any duties of a Coast Guard cutter, including arrest. More particularly, though, it is to the nation's requirements for military readiness that training in sailing ships generally, and *Eagle* particularly, is dedicated.

In a recent report to the superintendent of the Academy from the commanding officer of *Eagle,* training and drill exercises are listed among activities conducted on board early in the sailing season:

Multi-Ship Exercises
    Tactical Maneuvering

GUNNEX and Weapons
    Pyrotechnics exercise

Ships and General Drills
    Man Overboard
    Abandon Ship

Lecture
    Firefighting and Compartmentation
    Honors and Ceremonies
    Message Format
    Boarding Officer
    Sextant adjustment and techniques

ISE Evolutions
    Man Overboard
    Boat Operations
    Precision Anchoring
    In-port Fire Drill

Training Encountered by Actual Operation
    Mast Investigations
    Accident Reports
    Personal Claims against government investigation

Fueling
Classified Operation
Low-Visibility Piloting

The list has harsh implications. The Coast Guard often has to step into troubles that are sinister as well as unfortunate, and *Eagle*'s status as a square-rigged sailing barque in no way excludes her from training cadets in an armed service. For, although all United States services have rigorous training programs, few exercises call so completely and steadily on the personal resources of an officer cadet as sailing a square-rigger does. *Eagle* carries much of the latest high-technology navigational, meteorolgical, and situation-simulating equipment found on up-to-date military vessels. Not even the most realistic simulation devices and programs, however, can match the real experience of a sailing ship's deck and tophamper in oceanic conditions in revealing the cadet's makeup and character. And then the ship nurtures the cadet's best in speed, precision, efficiency, and, finally, prudence. Few military training programs offer such a combination of public visibility and demand for critical skills and personal responsibility as that presented to a square-rigger cadet. Beyond simulation, the ship presents real, immediate conditions directly connected to the well-being of the ship and her entire company, much in advance of the ostensibly similar training aboard engine-powered ships of the line. Captain Bill Earle relates a conversation with Captain Martin J. Moynihan, commanding officer of *Eagle* from 1980 to 1983:

> Marty put it succinctly. "With our cutter fleet reduced and only about twelve percent of our Coast Guard Officer Corps serving at sea, we need *Eagle* more than ever," he said. "This is the only place we can still make sailors."
>
> I agreed completely. True, the Coast Guard today needs fewer seamen. But it still needs *good* ones, people who can go in harm's way on the oceans and perform professionally. The nature of our business requires this. Despite burgeoning bureaucracy, we must continue to incubate a genuine deep-water sailor bloodline in our Officer Corps. Given the restrictions on numbers of cadets and diversity of Coast Guard duties, *Eagle* is the best possible vessel for doing this.

Coast Guard cadets go right into service after graduation, and the possibility of combat is always present even while on duty aboard *Eagle*. Though a training vessel, *Eagle* shall "go in harm's way" when called. *Eagle* is a school-ship barque, and also a cutter.

Eagle's Spirit — The Esprit de Corps

In spite of *Eagle*'s serious purpose, you will not be shocked to hear that sailing is fun. Even in the heyday of sail, of press gangs and bucko mates, of wooden ships and iron men, mariners used the water for pleasure as well as for their living. Merchant and military mariners alike would race their

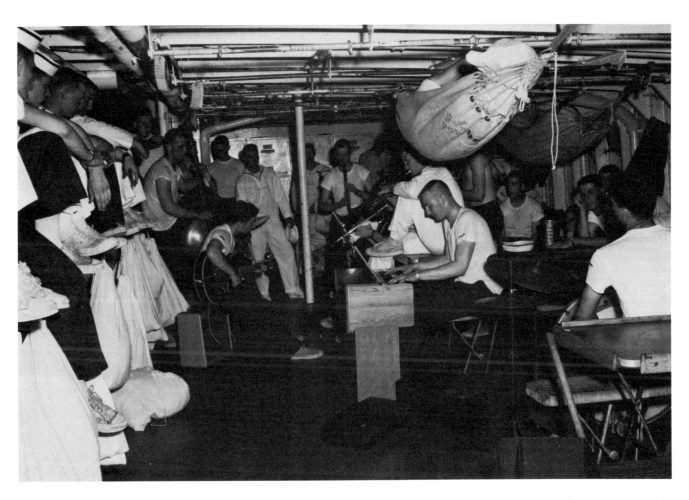

With changes in curriculum and the service's professional requirements, this scene in the berthing area of the old days is less common today. Still, jam sessions do happen, with a guitar or two on the foc'sle deck. Occasionally a band forms on the waist deck, weather permitting. (U.S Coast Guard Academy Archives photo)

ship's boats, yawls, and gigs; schooner fishermen would race their dories under both oar and sail; and of course aristocrats have taken their pleasures aboard yachts since ancient times. A fine boat, after all, is a thing of beauty, an elegant, functional sculpture that moves with dynamic grace. Except in high winds and heavy seas, aquatic motion is pleasant and relaxing. Boating in our period of history is available for simple pleasure to more people than ever before.

Much of the enjoyment of small craft carries over to sailing ships. The physics of a sailing vessel renders its motion much gentler and more predictable than that of a powered vessel of the same size and displacement. The wind in the sails is a steadying as well as a motive force, and it is quieter. The sounds are of wind in the rigging, and the seas surging along the hull, rather then the monotonous drone and vibration of internal combustion engines. For a ship that is both beautiful and a good sailor, her crew and company soon develop genuine affection. Mariners everywhere are yachtsmen of a kind. And a ship loved so well spreads her reputation — a farm family from, say, Iowa or Tennessee will drive or fly all the way to the coast, any coast, to observe a tall-ships event and *Eagle*.

If the entire Coast Guard Service refers to *Eagle* as "our" ship, imagine how personnel assigned aboard her feel! It is common for commissioned

Without the modern stripe or today's dress-white uniforms, Eagle *cuts a fine pre-1976 figure in harbor-furl and wharfside elegance. Here she is moored at the Washington Navy Yard in August 1962, awaiting the arrival of President John F. Kennedy for the ceremony pictured on page 91. (U.S. Coast Guard photo)*

officers to pass up other very desirable assignments for the possibility of a billet on the ship, and their ultimate disembarking and muster back ashore constitutes a genuine sadness, certainly the end of a personal era for the disenfranchised Coast Guardsman. Yet for them, forever afterward, *Eagle* remains "my" ship.

Some of *Eagle*'s sister vessels among the class A tall ships are perhaps equally fine sailors, with crews just as capable. But the especially happy resonances aboard *Eagle* are often remarked by skippers of the other ships. Again, Captain Earle:

> Each *Eagle* alumnus has his favorite story, often embellished with passage of time. Mine — unembellished — is of a black rainy night in 1954 when we were sailing close-hauled along the coast of Denmark trying to make the Skagerrak. A violent squall and sudden wind shift at midnight found us driving toward World War II mined areas, marked DANGER on the chart. All hands tumbled out in varying stages of undress to the strident "Stations for Stays" alarm. "Take in all sail!" was the order from the bridge. Though it seemed pandemonium, within minutes headsails and staysails were run down, yards settled, squaresails clewed up, spanker brailed in. Elmer coughed on the line and we thought we were through. But no — *Eagle* couldn't motor into the strong wind with those huge squaresails slatting in their gear. "Lay aloft and Furl!" Officers, cadets and crewmen alike scrambled aloft. I found a place on the main royal yard. The wind was howling, the sail thrashing like a wild thing. We beat it, fisted it, rolled up a hasty sea furl, and passed the gaskets. Dark figures on yards below were doing the same. Soon Elmer commenced throbbing purposefully and we felt the full blast of rain and wind in our faces. *Eagle* had turned upwind and was motoring clear of the danger.
>
> As we edged our way in to the mast, the cadet next to me on the footrope exclaimed, "Hey, that was fun!" Fun? I thought. A flap of that sail could have thrown both of us into the sea, some 130 feet down. "It was for the birds," I muttered. In the darkness, I didn't know who he was and he didn't know who I was — but we shared something that night neither of us will ever forget.

Across the decades these same notes ring: trained skills, challenge, duty, and fun.

Eagle Leadership 6

Eagle is host to a kind of cosmopolitanism, a sense that indeed the world is small, that no matter how many surprises it contains, none are out of reach. In the wardroom, proof of this spirit is evident, and many cadets express their full expectation that commissions will soon see them off to many quarters of the world in a direct and involved way. Few people aboard *Eagle* would ever call any place at sea no place. Fewer still would call foreign or unfamiliar domestic places inferior or unimportant. In training leaders, *Eagle* is a leader in showing us that the world does not stop at our shorelines.

In our history of the ship we described how it is part and parcel of *Eagle*'s tradition to go places. For thirty years it was in her ordinary course of duty to go to Europe, and some of the better-known *Eagle* literature, most notably that by Alan Villiers, describes her sea roads during that era. In more recent times, changes in Coast Guard Academy policy, and the need to completely refurbish the ship, have called for shorter voyages. This interim period ends in 1987, when *Eagle* sails the Pacific basin, beginning with a passage to Australia. Meanwhile her adventures closer to home have maintained the practice of rewarding her sailors with exotic places, serving too as ambassador from the United States, and demonstrating to young cadets the breadth of world experience.

It need not be Europe. St. Pierre and Miquelon are perfectly adequate, or Bermuda, or Canadian ports. After days at sea, the land is raised. The rail is lined with all hands who are not on watch. The chart speaks the truth. We are someplace else, and came under sail the entire distance.

New and different places. Why? After all, this is a training vessel; school is school, why the gilding on the lily? First, other countries invite *Eagle* to visit, as a mutual government courtesy, an expression of friendship, both ways, and good will toward citizens, people to people. Then, officer cadets are young people, facing large responsibilities in a large world, and the more they can learn about the world as students, the better. They have to face the challenge of the sea; let's introduce them to some of the challenges of the land, in strange places where they do not have a cultural upper hand.

With all sails set, Eagle *takes your breath away. This photo, often used by the Coast Guard Academy as an official portrait, remains visually special. The setting is New York harbor; the time is 1979. Governors Island and Coast Guard Third District Headquarters can be seen in the background. (U.S. Coast Guard photo by Neil Ruenzel)*

Awareness too that we are responsible for our national coast, and maintain it with a federal Coast Guard, demands of us consciousness of world intercourse, commerce, and communication. All the Coast Guard's duties — protecting revenues, maintaining aids to navigation, safeguarding coastal marine life and property, and intervening in any conditions that threaten American maritime interests — all imply interaction with others. Cadet officers need to experience other lands. Under sail, the routine destinations bring the ship's company naturally and inexpensively to foreign shores.

Eagle's ambassadorial status is unique in the Coast Guard service. Coast Guard craft and vessels usually have duty restricted to prescribed waters (great or small, depending on the size and function of the vessel) served by their base. *Eagle's* base is of course the Academy at New London, but her mission frees her from territorial restrictions, a natural advantage for a training ship. Training is enhanced by variety in the kinds of waters that she can sail: warm, cold, rough, foggy, heavily trafficked, and so on. But where she sails makes no great difference, and ports-of-call love having *Eagle* grace their waterfronts; invitations pour into Academy offices all the time. Coast Guard cadets are bound to serve on *Eagle,* and *Eagle* is bound to visit interesting places. A fine dose of cosmopolitanism is inherent in the sail-training experience.

Because of changed curriculum in recent years, the refitting and refurbishing schedule of the early 1980s, and perhaps, too, more restricted

A special panoramic camera presents Eagle *at her ambassadorial task, wharfside in Montreal in 1978.* (U.S. Coast Guard Academy photo)

Traditional Eagle, *all-seeing blimp, and futuristic space shuttle* Columbia *converge on display at the World's Fair in New Orleans in 1984.* Eagle's *daily communication at sea with aircraft and satellites spans the ages and technologies in her mission of training future Coast Guard officers.* (Ed Daniels photo)

service budgets, the annual transatlantic passages to Europe that seemed habitual for three decades have been curtailed. Southern, West Indian, and Canadian ports have been the general bill of fare, and no interocean journeys are planned for the ship until 1988, when *Eagle* will cross the South Pacific to Australia and probably other destinations around the Pacific. The West Coast has not seen its Coast Guard barque in almost a decade, and so its turn is coming soon again. Still, a half dozen municipal harbors enjoy the ship each sailing season, giving the local citizens an opportunity to step aboard a square-rigged sailing ship, and the cadets the experience of liberty in unfamiliar places.

Large sailing ships have always seemed romantic, but in the forty years since Captain McGowan brought *Eagle* to America, it long appeared that the romance and heritage of sailing ships was going to pass into oblivion, into mere quaint curiosity. *Eagle* of course had her value as a training vessel, but as two generations who recalled the last years of the great sailing era died, the future of large sailing ships turned bleak.

Perhaps because of modern boat construction and rigging, with hulls of glass-reinforced plastic, with synthetic rope and spars of extruded metal, or perhaps from simple nostalgia, in the early sixties interest in the traditional ships and ways of the sea awakened. Operation Sail celebrations began to attract attention, and the skippers and administrations for sail-training vessels worldwide began a vast network of correspondence and plans to coordinate their activities, so that from time to time several of

Pyrotechnics burst in celebration through Eagle's *tophamper at the World's Fair opening festivities in New Orleans, 1984. The ship's work is ordinarily at sea, but few forget seeing fireworks and a tall ship's rigging in the same view.* (Ed Daniels photo)

them could appear together and so create the splendid view a tall-ships event provides. Two or three of the twenty or so class A tall ships would appear together to help a city celebrate an anniversary, a fair, a famous yacht race. More countries began to show interest in participating. As the public's enthusiasm for sailing ships increased, so further involvement grew, until, in the wonderful Bicentennial Op-Sail display in 1976, tall ships registered indelibly in the public mind, and in another way in the minds of sailing-ship enthusiasts.

Most Americans who were adults or nearly so on July 4, 1976, remember where they were and what they did with whom on the nation's 200th birthday. On the public side, years of planning had gone into the event, and

A city's flotilla turns out for Eagle's *arrival, as here in Long Beach, California, in 1978. On these marvelous occasions, both cadets on* Eagle *and admirers who make the effort to stand by and salute the ship will long recall being there.* (U.S. Coast Guard Academy photo)

the Coast Guard was not idle. Not only would the many harbor celebrations require marine traffic planning, monitoring, and patrol, but the service itself wanted to make a statement in honor of the event — to recognize its past, and to use the time to announce its full participation in the future. It painted a distinctive slash on *Eagle's* hull similar to that which has graced the hulls of other Coast Guard ships and boats since 1967. This decoration accomplished many things, including ease of recognition of Coast Guard ships and boats on the nation's waters. It also aroused aesthetic doubts within the nautical fraternity. Some people thought it clever and liked it. Many deplored it and, thinking of *Eagle,* skirted the brink of apoplexy.

The debut for *Eagle's* stripe was the July 4 Op-Sail '76 event in New York, up to that time the largest fleet of class A tall ships ever assembled, sixteen in all, with another thirty class B vessels in attendance as well. Traditionalists were aghast. Everyone else noticed that they had no trouble at all recognizing which was the U.S. ship. Most of those opinions became instantly fixed, never to be moved. Nevertheless, a decade has smoothed the debate: the service planned to modify the stripes by removing the words Coast Guard, and the traditionalists voluntarily cultivated flawed eyesight. You can easily tell *Eagle* from her sisters, anyway.

Whereas twenty years ago marine and nautical museums languished, today they blossom with programs and excellent teaching exhibits and watercraft development schemes. Several cities have commissioned and built their own sail-training and ambassadorial vessels, and others announce intentions to do so almost monthly. And everywhere, harborside waterfront areas that in recent memory were seedy and rundown places are now among the most desirable properties and residential areas of which a city can brag. As the carrier and embodiment of maritime tradition and pride, *Eagle,* the only working square-rigged vessel owned by the United States, has helped lead in this national, indeed international,

The Five Sisters' Cup, raced for whenever a quorum can be gathered, which is never often enough for lovers of tall ships. This is the silver through which sailors in five bottoms find hard work and well-earned glory. Eagle, Sagres II, Tovarishch, Mircea, *and* Gorch Fock II *are the five sisters. The cup is presently in* Gorch Fock II's *flag cabin.*

Ship's visitors are of many styles and sizes; these bode well for America's maritime future. Fort Lauderdale, Florida, 1984. (U.S. Coast Guard photo)

Op-Sail 1976, New York Harbor, Statue of Liberty presiding. The gracious lady celebrates her one hundredth birthday, and Eagle *her fiftieth, in 1986.* (U.S. Coast Guard photo)

rediscovery of things marine. With ambassadorial appearances not interrupting but enhancing the ship's training functions, clouds of canvas on harbor horizons promise to be a permanent feature of the urban marine environment.

Any harbor graced by two or more of the ships will have, along with the spectacle, fine society between the ships, great fun sharing experiences and trading souvenirs, and lowered language and cultural barriers. Music and a bit of dancing are not unknown at such times, and such a time was summer 1984, when *Eagle* tied up at a pier in Québec across from *Kruzenshtern,* the Soviet Union's 375-foot four-masted barque. Youthful sailors being who they are, glances, nods, and waves soon evolved into conversations and ship tours, then singalongs and genuine camaraderie. It all happened so quickly that political officers (one officer in four) aboard the Soviet vessel were caught aback, and for a time seemed intimidated by the escalating hilarity of the proceedings. Eventually they brought an end to it by signaling a ship's muster, and removing themselves out into the roadstead at anchor. Several days later, when for ceremonial reasons the two crews again found themselves in company, it was a very different Russian crew; somber, reticent, thoroughly chastised. Nevertheless *Eagle* cadets and crew did catch a secret glance, wink, or smirk, devious and brief.

When *Eagle* casts her lines and comes to wharfside on official visits, she shows another distinction that has also become traditional: gracious hospi-

tality. The regular cadet watches are set, and go on as usual, but now some spit-and-polish is added, as the ladies and gentlemen become hosts. Millions of people have walked *Eagle*'s deck, craning in wonder at the rigging aloft, touching the varnished brightwork and polished brass. Among them have been mayors and officials from scores of cities, a half-dozen presidents of the United States, kings and queens, renowned world leaders in government, religion, education, the arts and sciences; all invited and gracefully received. Young people who twenty-four hours before might

An avid navy man and sailor, Prince Philip of Great Britain tours the below-decks of Eagle *in 1957. England, to the chagrin of British sailing-ship enthusiasts, has no class A tall ship of its own.* (U.S. Coast Guard Academy Museum photo)

Admiral James S. Gracey, commandant of the United States Coast Guard, greets Canada's Prime Minister Pierre Trudeau aboard Eagle. *Such times on the ship honor everyone who participates. Quebec, 1984.* (U.S. Coast Guard photo by Doug Bandos)

have battled slatting canvas a hundred feet over the sea in a rain squall in the middle of the night find themselves now official receptionists in the care not only of a ship, but of a service, a nation, an idea before all who would come aboard; a family on holiday, a U.S. Senator, personnel from another service, a television crew, a marine historical society, and on and on. Everyone is welcome, and in these official receptions, no society columnist could find reason for complaint. *Eagle*'s galley team puts on a spread that would not embarrass any salon. Of the many hundreds of receptions *Eagle* has held over the years, one that came in mid-career featured a particularly nautical president and memorable human circumstances.

In 1962, out of the Canary Islands and homeward bound from Europe, *Eagle* received word that the ship was to proceed to Chesapeake Bay and the Potomac River, there to receive President John F. Kennedy. On arrival, hospitality was tendered to the Commander-in-Chief, as the ship had in the past, and would again several times in ensuing years. A Navy man and a sailor, Kennedy was particularly effusive in praising the ship and the Coast Guard service. His address was flattering and sincere, and his pleasure in the occasion was evident, for he lingered to talk to the ship's crew, man-to-man. Among the chief petty officers he met John F. Kennedy, and the president was charmed. Next to Mr. Kennedy in the receiving line was First Class Petty Officer John Paul Jones, a salty professional Coast Guardsman. The president was delighted. Third in line was First Class Petty Officer Robert Louis Stephenson. The multiple coincidence was a hit.

In 1986 *Eagle* is fifty years old, a veteran known to cadets as the Great White Bird, and coming to know her one may hear some of the hundreds of stories about life on board. Over the years she has been relatively gentle to herself and her charges, but with more than 4,000 cadets trained, and hundreds of thousands of sea miles sailed, fate has occasionally taken its toll. In forty years, three crew deaths have occurred, one ship collision cost her a bowsprit, and now and then a dock or wharf has been nudged hard in a few minor crashes. Despite some weather emergencies and a mishap here and there, for a ship of her size and complement, and youthful, inexperienced people aboard her, *Eagle* has a remarkable record for safety and successful missions. As Plato said, there is no learning without pain, but *Eagle* has generally experienced learning pains only in drills and qualification deadlines. In countless gales and a couple of genuine hurricanes the ship did exactly what she was supposed to do: get everyone through them, and teach young mariners respect for the sea.

Seamanship is the primary focus of *Eagle*'s mission, and she is, in effect, on station whenever and wherever she is at sea. She has come to the aid of a few distressed boats, taking them in tow or otherwise giving succor, and yet she has arrived at the scene of some marine disasters hours too late, though every effort was made to be there in time.

The *Andrea Doria* tragedy had left nothing but flotsam by the time she got there. In 1984, *Eagle*'s position 100 miles north of *Marques* prevented her from helping. She has helped clean up no oil or chemical spills, and has never acted as a lightship or tended a buoy. She has not acted as icebreaker or conducted surveillance over icebergs or drug smugglers. She has never

Roots author Alex Haley enjoys some maritime heritage aboard Eagle. *Earlier* Eagles *were active in battles against the slave trade.* (U.S. Coast Guard photo)

John F. Kennedy greets the president of the United States aboard Eagle, *with his fellow crew members John Paul Jones and Robert Louis Stephenson (only his First Class Petty Officer sleeve showing) in attendance. The president was charmed by the event, and much impressed by* Eagle. *Washington Navy Yard, August 1962. (U.S. Coast Guard photo)*

engaged in a boat-safety inspection, or heaved to and examined a foreign fishing trawler's hold and catch to see that it complied with treaty laws. But her officers and enlisted men have done all these, and her cadets will certainly do so.

Now and then, however, fate places all deep-water vessels in the way of danger and the call to service. During the autumn 1985 short cruise to Bermuda, for example, *Eagle* received a distress call from the sailing vessel *Sunshine* over channel 16 VHF/FM, a standard monitor frequency over radio equipment generally used by small craft plying inshore waters

— not in deep-sea duty. The yacht was about 75 miles north northwest of Bermuda, and *Eagle* about 26 miles north of the yacht's position. Conditions were frightful for a 43-foot sailing sloop, with ten-foot seas and winds to forty knots, and both increasing. Indeed, *Eagle*'s shortened sail and tremendous windage aloft had her own speed through the water down to little more than one knot under the prevailing circumstances.

Sunshine had been underway from New York to the Virgin Islands for five days, in dirty weather the entire time, her inexperienced crew exhausted on a boat without a life raft, no extra sails, existing sails that could not be "shortened" for high winds, very limited communications ability, and only five running hours worth of fuel remaining, in a rapidly worsening gale. When admonished to change course toward *Eagle*, *Sunshine*'s master declined, insisting on a rhumb line toward Bermuda. Discovering that Bermuda had neither towing nor fueling vessels available to go to assistance under the conditions involved, *Sunshine* was finally persuaded by *Eagle* to alter course. No other vessels could be located in the vicinity. It was up to *Eagle*.

Because a rather large portion of *Eagle*'s complement was composed of inexperienced trainees, a special effort was made to brief and instruct the crew on rescue equipment and procedures, especially those for towing vessels at sea. Meanwhile, extra lookouts were posted, and as night began to fall (about 7:00 P.M. on October 23, 1985), a series of flare launchings was initiated to locate the sailboat. All hands were called on deck to scan the view through the rain- and spume-filled murk. *Sunshine* was sighted on the second flare launching.

Thus began a series of near-misses and mishaps, all due to the inexperience of the crew aboard the yacht. The helmsman had to be continually cautioned about not approaching *Eagle* too closely and so fouling the boat's rigging with the ship's. Then, when *Eagle*'s crew had cast a "messenger" (a light throwing line cast over another craft and used to haul aboard a proper towing hawser), the yacht's crew simply made the messenger fast to the yacht's forebits, an arrangement distinctly not up to the task at hand. The wind was howling, the seas were high and quick, and both boat and ship were pitching and rolling in the steep seas. Visibility was bad, hearing almost nonexistent. In the process of maneuvering to avoid a foul aloft, *Sunshine* (still not understanding the purpose of the messenger) allowed the light line to go slack, and it quickly became fouled in the yacht's rudderpost and propeller, thus placing the boat in severe danger of capsizing.

Eagle backed down to keep by the now-helpless yacht — a procedure very difficult for a sailing barque under these conditions of sea and wind. Against all shipboard judgment and advice, one of the yacht's crew crawled down over the boat's transom in an attempt to clear the line fouling the yacht's rudder and prop, a large sea nearly taking him. Finally, another messenger was passed and a proper hawser secured to the sailboat. The next day things became even worse, with winds to 55 knots and seas to more than 15 feet, ship and tow making bare headway of any kind, and making any attempt to remove the crew from the stricken boat extremely risky. When, finally, *Eagle* determined to place a trained sailing crew aboard the yacht (all Coast Guard Academy graduates receive thorough training in all manner of sailing boats, including yacht hulls), conditions began to moderate. Speed improved, and routine passage to Bermuda, with tow, was completed.

Later investigation and briefing concluded that the yacht would likely have perished if not for its encounter with *Eagle*.

Eagle has many sea stories to tell. This one is told here because it is recent, and more particularly because it is so very typical of the jams into which pleasure craft can get themselves when they are poorly managed and under-equipped — the results of which the Coast Guard must deal with all the time. For the ship, the event was a log entry and briefing. For the officers and crew it was the usual old-hat confusion of sea rescue. For the young cadets, it was their first crack at their chosen duty.

Eagle seems destined to do her regular work. Now and again she receives a special assignment, which is easily taken in stride, because of the long and short cruises her regular duty requires. For calls to special service, the work is simply integrated with established plans, as in 1975 when *Eagle* was dispatched to Lubec, Maine, to pick up and deliver to the Academy in New London the bones of Hopley Yeaton.

An able, canny, somewhat political man, Yeaton was the first fully commissioned cutter master in the Revenue Marine Service under Alexander Hamilton's Treasury and George Washington's administration. As a correspondent of Hamilton's, he had been forewarned of plans for a revenue service and so made sure to be in Washington's good graces. Thus he was readily confirmed when Treasury recommendations were submitted. His ship, out of Portsmouth, New Hampshire, and assigned to the down-East Machias station, was not the first launched, but his was the first commission to oversee building and assume mastership. For this reason the *Yeaton* name has been carried by Great Guard cutters for years.

Yeaton died and was interred in East Lubec, Maine, in 1808, having remained in the service until his death. There he rested until, in 1975, permission was secured to disinter his remains and remove them under honor guard aboard *Eagle,* thence to New London by sea, and finally from the ship to the Academy chapel grounds, where his role in the early history of the United States Coast Guard could be properly honored. Captain James Heydenreich's research and efforts to see this fascinating man properly recognized would make a worthwhile book.

But such events involving sea duty for cadets bring to mind worries in the officer ranks about *Eagle* becoming squeezed between ambassadorial and publicity chores, on the one hand, and too much distraction of cadets while they are on board because of their professional requirements, on the other hand. Alumni of the ship wonder if today's cadets get enough relaxed time, simply to be with ship and shipmates, sea and sky. When in the 1950s Alain Villiers said of *Eagle*:

> The revival of the square rigger under the American flag stands as a
> great Coast Guard achievement, made possible by the exceptional

merit of its officers, its great traditions, and its plain hard-working guts

the times were not so pressed by the welter of high technology and paperwork. Now that only 12 percent of the Coast Guard serves at sea, the possibility grows that a distinction will be made between courage and brains, an insidious one for seagoers. For all the reknown of an Op-Sail event, and the gracious value of calling on a port city and its luminaries, the vessel's true place is at sea, doing her job with a full complement of cadets.

For the sailing-ship enthusiast, knowing that *Eagle* is out there somewhere, sailing, is satisfaction enough. If in these pages you have picked up a taste of the romance, you will see the justification for a publicly owned sailing barque. *Eagle* is *our* ship, yours and mine. See her when you can, stand on her decks, and know that the core of our maritime heritage is thriving.

In that difficult winter of 1946, when Captain McGowan was amidst the desperate job of fitting out this splendid barque of ours, one day he found himself over coffee, talking to the kapitanleutnant, former skipper of the ship, across a very sturdy language barrier. It had just been learned that

In this photo taken from the U.S.C.G.C. Alert, *U.S. Secretary of Transportation Drew Lewis salutes in the Coast Guard commandant's change-of-command ceremonies at the Washington Navy Yard, May 1982. From left to right: incoming Admiral James S. Gracey, outgoing Admiral John B. Hayes, and Secretary Lewis. (U.S. Coast Guard photo)*

(Ed Daniels photo)

Through Eagle's *rigging, we watch the space shuttle* Discovery's *launching from Cape Canaveral, June 1985.* (Ed Daniels photo)

the ship's name was to be *Eagle*. The German officer looked a little confused. "Igles?" he said; that means, how you say, "hedgehog." The captain was quick to correct the impression; no, it was *Eagle, Adler* in German. "Ah," the vanquished officer said, "that is a *very good* name indeed!"

Appendix I

Eagle Itinerary, 1946–present

The following list of ports-of-call in *Eagle*'s cruise history does not include many short cruises and special courtesy stopover calls that have always been part of the ship's responsibilities. Only the primary training cruises of each season are listed.

1946: Martha's Vineyard, Nantucket, New Bedford (all in Massachusetts)

1947: Bermuda; Caneel Bay, Virgin Islands; San Juan, Puerto Rico; Nassau, Bahamas; Miami, Florida; Coral Gables, Florida; Parris Island, South Carolina; Norfolk, Virginia; New York City

1948: Ponta Delgada, Azores; London, England; Le Havre, France; Santa Cruz, Canary Islands; Bermuda

1949: London, England; Antwerp, Belgium; Lisbon, Portugal; Casablanca, Morocco; Santa Cruz, Canary Islands

1950: Amsterdam, The Netherlands; Antwerp, Belgium; La Coruña, Spain; Lisbon, Portugal; Madeiras

1951: London and Portsmouth, England; Antwerp, Belgium; Amsterdam, The Netherlands; Le Havre, France; Lisbon, Portugal; Casablanca, Morocco; Canary Islands; Halifax, Nova Scotia; Bermuda

1952: Oslo, Norway; Copenhagen, Denmark; Amsterdam, The Netherlands; Santander, Spain; Tenerife, Canary Islands; Bermuda

1953: Oslo, Norway; Antwerp, Belgium; Santander, Spain; Las Palmas, Canary Islands

1954: Santander, Spain; Amsterdam, The Netherlands; Copenhagen, Denmark; Bermuda

1955: Glasgow, Scotland; Le Havre, France; Lisbon, Portugal; Madeiras; Bermuda

1956: San Juan, Puerto Rico; Coco Solo, Panama Canal Zone; Havana, Cuba; Halifax, Nova Scotia

1957: Bergen, Norway; London, England; La Coruña, Spain

1958: Amsterdam, The Netherlands; Dublin, Ireland; Lisbon, Portugal; Halifax, Nova Scotia

1959: San Juan, Puerto Rico; Ciudad Trujillo; Willemstad, Curacao; Kingston, Jamaica; Gardiners Bay, New York; Québec City, Québec; Nantucket, Massachusetts; Provincetown, Massachusetts

1960:   Oslo, Norway; Portsmouth, England; Le Havre, France

1961:   Bordeaux, France; Lisbon, Portugal; Cadiz, Spain; Santa Cruz de Tenerife, Canary Islands

1962:   Edinburgh, Scotland; Antwerp, Belgium; Las Palmas, Canary Islands; Washington, D.C.; Yorktown, Virginia; Bermuda

1963:   Oslo, Norway; Amsterdam, The Netherlands; Santander, Spain; Funchal, Azores; Madeira

1964:   San Juan, Puerto Rico; Bermuda; New York City; Québec City, Québec; Bermuda

1965:   Miami, Florida; Panama City, Panama; Acapulco, Mexico; Long Beach, California; Seattle, Washington; San Francisco, California; San Diego, California

1966:   Wilmington, North Carolina; Boston, Massachusetts

1967:   Montreal, Québec; Cape May, New Jersey; Providence, Rhode Island; Nantucket, Massachusetts

1968:   New York City; Provincetown, Massachussetts; Portsmouth, New Hampshire; Yorktown, Virginia; Hamilton, Bermuda

1969:   Norfolk, Virginia; New York City; Portland, Maine; Newport, Rhode Island

1970:   Southport, North Carolina; Portsmouth, Virginia; New York City; Newport, Rhode Island

1971:   St. George, Bermuda; Boston, Massachusetts; Portsmouth, New Hampshire; Newburyport, Massachusetts

1972:   Mobile, Alabama; New Orleans, Louisiana; Galveston, Texas; Portsmouth, England; Lubec, West Germany; Travelmunde and Keil, West Germany; Lisbon, Portugal; Madeira

1973:   Boston, Massachusetts; San Juan, Puerto Rico; Port Everglades, Florida; Charleston, South Carolina; New Bedford, Massachusetts; Newburyport, Massachusetts; Philadelphia, Pennsylvania

1974:   Washington, D.C.; St. George, Bermuda; Newport, Rhode Island; Boston, Massachusetts; New York City; Portsmouth, New Hampshire; New Bedford, Massachusetts

1975:   Antwerp, Belgium; Le Havre, France; Rota, Spain; Malaga, Spain; Funchal, Maderia

1976:   Philadelphia, Pennsylvania; Alexandria, Virginia; Bermuda; Newport, Rhode Island; New York City; Baltimore, Maryland; Jacksonville and Miami, Florida; Charleston, South Carolina; New Bedford, Massachusetts

1977:   Hamburg, West Germany; London, England; Rota, Spain

1978:   Guantanamo, Cuba; Cristobal, Panama; Acapulco, Mexico; San Diego, California; Victoria, British Columbia; Vancouver, British Columbia; Seattle, Washington; San Francisco and Long Beach, California

1979:   Halifax, Nova Scotia; Norfolk, Virginia; Washington, D.C.; New York City; Bermuda; Savannah, Georgia

1980:   Boston, Massachusetts; St. Thomas, Virgin Islands; San Juan, Puerto Rico; Barbados; St. Lucia; Santo Domingo, Dominican Republic; St. Petersburg, Florida; Miami, Florida; Charleston, South Carolina

1981: Cork, Ireland; Lisbon, Portugal; Rota, Spain; Malaga, Spain; Las Palmas, Canary Islands; Bermuda; New Haven, Connecticut

1982: Washington, D.C.; Norfolk, Virginia; Philadelphia, Pennsylvania; Newport, Rhode Island; New York City; Portland, Maine

1983: Port of Spain, Trinidad; St. Thomas; Roosevelt Roads, Puerto Rico; Port Everglades, Florida; Bermuda

1984: New Orleans, Louisiana; Halifax, Nova Scotia; Québec City, Québec; Portsmouth, New Hampshire; Bourne, Massachusetts

1985: Cape Canaveral, Florida; Mobile, Alabama; Jacksonville, Florida; Bermuda; Boston, Massachusetts, St. Pierre et Miquelon; New Bedford, Massachusetts; Gloucester, Massachusetts

1986: Yorktown, Virginia; Hamilton, Bermuda; Washington, D.C.; Hamilton, Bermuda; Norfolk, Virginia; New York City (for Op-Sail and Liberty Weekend '86); Halifax, Nova Scotia; Newport, Rhode Island; Portland, Maine; Portsmouth, New Hampshire

Appendix II

List of *Eagle* commanding officers

Kommandanten *Horst Wessel:*

Kapitan August Thiele, 1936–38
Korvettenkapitan Weyher, January 1939–September 1939
Kapitanleutnant Kretschmar, March 1940–May 1940
Fregattenkapitan Eiffe, March 1941–November 1942
Kapitanleutnant Schnibbe, November 1942–May 1945

Commanders U.S.C.G. barque *Eagle:*

Captain Gordon P. McGowan, 1946–47
Captain Miles Imlay, 1947–48
Captain Carl B. Olsen, 1949
Captain Carl B. Bowman, 1950–54
Captain Karl O.A. Zittel, 1954–58
Captain William B. Ellis, 1959
Captain Chester I. Steele, 1960–61
Captain Robert A. Schulz, 1961–62
Captain William A. Earle, 1963–65
Captain Peter A. Morrill, 1965 west coast–east coast ferry run
Captain Archibald B. How, 1965–67
Captain Stephen G. Carkeek, 1967
Commander Harold A. Paulsen, 1968–71
Captain Edward D. Cassidy, 1972–73
Captain James C. Irwin, 1974–75
Captain James R. Kelly, 1975–76
Captain Paul A. Welling, 1976–80
Captain Martin J. Moynihan, 1980–83
Captain Ernst M. Cummings, 1983–

Appendix III

Glossary

aft, abaft, after: In, near, or toward the stern of a vessel.

alee: On or toward the lee, the side of a ship that is away from the wind.

aloft: Above the deck of a ship; in the rigging.

amidships: In or toward the middle of a ship; midway between the bow and stern.

anchor windlass: A mechanical device used to hoist a ship's anchor by its cable.

athwartships: At right angles to the fore-and-aft line of a vessel; *across* a vessel.

ballast: Heavy material placed low in ships to maintain proper stability, trim, or draft.

Baltimore clipper: A name formerly given in the United States to a sharp-bow built schooner or brig-rigged vessel with a tonnage from 90 to 200 tons. The masts were given a great amount of rake in order to preserve a proper balance of sail; the hull had great dead rise and cutaway ends. The length was 35 to 120 feet on deck. The type is now obsolete.

beam: The width of a ship. Also called *breadth.*

berth (also: berthing): The shelf-like space allotted to a passenger or member of the crew as a sleeping place.

billet: A berth or duty assignment, usually on a military ship.

bitt: Any of the deck posts, often in pairs, around which lines or cables are wound and may be made fast.

block: A mechanical contrivance consisting of one or more grooved pulleys mounted in a casing or shell fitted with a hook, eye, or strap by which it may be attached.

boarding seas: Waves large enough to come on board the deck of a ship.

boatswain (also: bos'n, bosun): A warrant grade deck officer on board a naval ship who has immediate charge of all boatswain's mates and seamen and is in control of all deck evolutions.

bos'n hole: Slang for boatswain's locker, a small compartment in which are stored tools and small items for repairing and making up rigging or other deck gear.

bow: The forward part or head of a vessel, more particularly above the waterline, beginning where the sides trend inward and terminating where they close or unite in the stem.

brace(s): Running rigging used to swing the yards in a horizontal plane.

brails: Lines used in furling the spanker to bring it into the mizzenmast.

breadth: The width of a ship, also called *beam.*

brig: A two-masted ship with square sails on both masts.

brow: A ship's "gangplank" for entry and exit between the ship and shore.

bulkhead: An upright partition separating parts of a ship, for protection against fire, flooding, etc.

bulwarks: The raised woodwork or plating running along each side of the vessel above the weather deck, helping to keep the decks dry, and serving also as a fence against losing deck cargo or men overboard.

captain's gig: A ship's small boat, *usually* reserved for the commanding officer.

chief: A chief engineer or chief officer in the merchant service; a chief petty officer in the U.S. Navy or Coast Guard.

chief petty officer: The highest of several noncommissioned ranks obtainable by enlisted personnel in the Coast Guard Service.

chock: A block with two hornlike projections curving inward through which a line may be run and for which it serves as a fairlead.

cleat: A small piece of wood or metal with projecting ends on which a line may be made fast.

clipper: A sharp-bowed, narrow-beamed sailing ship (c. 1830s) built for great speed.

clipper bow: Bow in which the stem forms a concave curve that projects outboard above the waterline. Also called *fiddle bow, cutwater bow, knee bow, overhanging bow.*

colors: A ship's national flag. The naval ceremony that takes place at hoisting of the colors at 8:00 A.M. and lowering at sunset.

compartmentation (subdivision): The partitioning of the hull's internal volume transversely and longitudinally into a number of compartments in order to reduce the quantity of water that may gain access to it through stranding, collision, or any other accidental cause.

complement: The number of crew employed upon a vessel for its safe navigation.

counter stern: A form of stern in which the upper works extend abaft the rudderpost, forming a continuation of the lines of the hull. Also called *overhanging stern.*

course: One of the square sails on the lowest yard of a square-rigged ship. The fore course–main course. The point of the compass on which a ship sails.

cutter: A fast, small ocean-going vessel, usually a government type (*e.g.,* Coast Guard) for patrolling and law-enforcement duties.

davits: A pair of cranes for hoisting and lowering a ship's boats.

deck: Principal component of the ship's structure, consisting of a planked or plated surface, approximately horizontal, extending between the ship's sides, and resting upon a tier of deck beams.

deck watch: The part of a ship's company that is employed in working it at one time.

depth sounder: An apparatus for measuring the depth of water by means of underwater sound vibrations sent out from the vessel.

dock: A large excavated basin equipped with floodgates, used for receiving ships between voyages. A water space between piers.

dogged: Any of several devices for holding, grappling, or securing a hatch, door, or gear.

draft (also: draught): The vertical depth of a vessel below the waterline.

drydock: A dock from which the water can be emptied, used for building and repairing ships.

ease: To pay out slowly and with care. Reduce strain on a line.

ensign: The flag carried by a ship as the insignia of her nationality.

evaporator: A heat-transfer device in the distilling plant that uses steam (usually auxiliary exhaust steam) to heat sea water. The resulting vapor is condensed in the distilling condensor to become fresh water to be used for boiler feed and general ship's use.

executive officer: One of the certificated members of the ship's staff who under the master's authority assists him in the operation of the vessel.

faking: To lay out line or chain on deck, for easy running or inspection.

fidley: An opening or trunkway immediately above a fireroom, having great width, through which boiler uptakes, lower stack, and fireroom ventilators are led. At the top deck or just above it is decked over with light plating. Small hatchways with grating covers are provided.

figurehead: A carved figure on the bow of a ship.

fitted-out: The conditioning and equipping of a ship for sea duty.

first class cadet: A cadet who is in his or her graduating or senior year at a service academy.

fittings: As used in marine insurance, this term covers the permanent equipment of a vessel, including that required for the particular trade in which she is engaged, the provisions for the crew, and the fuel and engine room stores.

flag cabin: A ship's cabin reserved specifically for the use of flag officers.

flag officer: Naval officer with the rank of rear admiral or above, so called because he is entitled to fly his personal flag that indicates his rank.

flax: Sail cloth made from flax fibers. Wearing qualities are superior to those of cotton sail cloth.

fo'c'sle deck: A phonetic spelling of forecastle deck.

forecastle deck: A term applied to a deck extending from the stem aft over a forecastle.

fore, forward: Term used chiefly in words denoting some parts of a ship's forward framing, equipment, or machinery that lies near the stem or in that direction, in contradistinction to *aft;* also, parts connected with the foremast.

fore truck: The very top of the foremast.

fore topmast: The section of mast extending above the foremast lower section.

freeboard: The vertical distance measured on the vessel's side amidships from the load waterline to the upper side of the freeboard deck or a point corresponding to it.

freeing ports: A rectangular or oval opening in the bulwarks, close to the deck and fitted with a flap cover that opens outward to allow water shipped on deck to run freely overboard.

furl: To fold up a sail to a yard, boom, mast, or stay and fasten it with a gasket to secure it snugly.

gallows post: A deck fitting designed to secure a boom.

gangway: An opening in the ship's side for loading and unloading freight or passengers.

gaskets: Small line, canvas strap, or plaited line employed to secure a sail to a yard, boom, or gaff when furled.

ground tackle: A general term for anchors, cables, warps, springs, and so on used for securing a vessel at anchor.

gyro, gyro compass, gyro repeater: An instrument receiving directive force from a gyroscope operated by electric motors that indicates a ship's true course.

hank(s): A ring of wood, metal, or rope that rides on a stay and to which the luff of a staysail or headsail is fastened.

hatch: An opening, generally rectangular, in a ship's deck affording access to the compartment below.

haul: To manually pull on a line or other running gear.

hawser: A large rope or line, generally used between vessels, as in towing.

hawser locker: A compartment in a ship where mooring lines or hawsers are stored.

headway: A vessel's motion forward or ahead.

heel: To lean to a side; slant, list, tilt over from force of wind or waves.

helm: The helm proper is the tiller, but the term is often used to mean the rudder and the gear for turning it. The word *helm* describes the whole steering apparatus in the form of rudder, tiller, chains, engine, wheel, telemotor, and so on.

helmsman: A person stationed at a ship's steering device.

hemp (tarred): Tall Asiatic plant of the nettle family, grown for its tough fiber. The fiber is used to make rope, etc. Often "tarred" in petroleum and tree-based oils or waxes so that it will "lay" or serve well in marlinspike (rope and line) applications, of which there are many.

hoist: Block and tackle or crane to raise aloft; lift or pull up, especially by means of a rope.

hulk: An old unseaworthy vessel, usually stripped of all her gear. A wreck.

LAN: Local Apparent Noon; the observed sun at the apex of its daily arc, its "fix" providing a navigational position, ship's latitude.

lay aloft, lay out: Order given to sailors up in the rigging to lay out on the yards; lay, to go there.

leeward: Situated on the side turned away from the wind as opposed to windward. Toward the lee.

let go and haul: A command given under sail in which the yards of the foremast are swung to the opposite tack when maneuvering under sail.

lifts: Wire rope and chain used for taking the weight of a yard, boom and enabling it to be topped or trimmed to the desired angle.

line: General term for ropes of different sizes used for various purposes on board ship.

lookout: Member of the crew stationed on the forecastle or aloft, whose duty it is to watch for any dangerous object lying near the ship's track, for any other vessel heaving in sight, and so on.

maintopmast: The section of the mast extending above the mainmast lower section.

making the colors: The setting of the ship's ensign and other attended flags. From "to make," to accomplish an act.

mallet: A hammer-shaped wooden implement used by sailmakers, wood-caulkers, riggers, shiprights. The head is made of wood, and the striking faces are ringed with iron.

manila line: Cordage made from the fibrous material contained in the leaves of the abaca plant and stronger than tarred hemp.

marlin: Two-stranded, lightly tarred hemp cord. It is commonly used for serving, lashings, mousings, and seizing stuff.

marlin spike: A pointed iron instrument for separating the strands of rope in splicing or marling.

mastcap: A collar used to confine two masts or spars together when one is erected at the head of another. It is made of wood, iron-bound, or built up of steel, and it has a square hole that fits over the lower masthead and a round one through which the mast above passes and is secured.

mess, messroom: A space or compartment in which members of the ship's company have their meals.

messenger: A general term for lines sent out to lead heavier lines, such as to lead mooring hawsers or towing hawsers.

mizzen truck: The uppermost portion of the mizzenmast.

muster: The assembling of the ship's company and passengers for inspection or drill.

oakum: Caulking material made of tarred yarn, used to waterproof seams between deck planking.

ordnance: Weaponry, especially guns, ammunition, or pyrotechnic flares.

packet: A small, fast sailing vessel used in coastwise trading and having a scheduled run.

peak tank: A ballast tank in the extreme bow or stern, used for trimming ship.

pelorus: Navigational instrument used for taking bearings, usually mounted outboard on a vertical stand, in the wings of the bridge on each side, or in some other convenient location.

plating: An external layer of metal plates attached to frames of a ship; "skin of a steel ship."

plotting; to plot: Laying down a course on a chart the position of a vessel or of a place or of the ship's course.

poop deck: A partial deck over the main deck at the stern.

port: The left-hand side of a ship as one faces forward, toward the bow.

preventer: An additional rope or wire fitted with tackle and attached to or placed alongside a heavily laden line, brace, or backstay to relieve effort and prevent accidents.

quarterdeck: Now an area on a naval vessel reserved for ceremonies and honors. Located on the ship wherever the commanding officer dictates.

ratlines: Any of the relatively small pieces of line that join the shrouds of a ship and serve as rungs for climbing the rigging.

ready boats: Small service boats kept in condition for immediate use; rigged out, over the side, hanging from davits, lashed into ship's rails.

reveille: A call on a pipe, bugle, drum, etc., at some time early in the morning to waken sailors or call them to first assembly.

revenue cutters: Seagoing vessels assigned to monitor marine traffic, especially in regard to the import of goods and the collection of import duties.

rhumb line: The course of a ship that keeps a constant compass direction, drawn as a line on a chart and globe and cutting across all meridians at the same angle.

rib(s) (frame): Any of the curved crosspieces extending from the keel to the top of the hull in a ship, forming its framework.

rig: The distinctive arrangement of sails, masts, shrouds, etc., on a vessel.

rigging screws (bottle): A device for adjustment of length fitted at the lower end of shrouds, stays, smokestack guys, and so on, in lieu of deadeyes and lanyards. See also *turnbuckle*.

righting moment: The moment of the righting couple that tends to restore a vessel to the upright when it has been inclined. It is expressed in foot-tons and equals the displacement of the vessel multiplied by the righting lever.

roadstead: A protected place near shore, not so enclosed as a harbor, where ships can ride safely at anchor.

sailcloth: Long-fibered canvas or other cloth used in making sails.

sailing auxiliaries: Sailing craft that also has engine power.

sailing master: Ship's officer in charge of sailing and seamanship operations.

SATNAV: Electronic navigation system via the interaction of shipboard equipment and satellites.

schooner: A ship with two or more masts, rigged fore and aft.

scupper(s): One of the drains set in decks to carry off accumulations of rain or sea water.

scuttled: To intentionally sink a ship by opening her sea cocks or cutting through the bottom.

sea cock: Valve fitted to the ship's hull plating. Used in flooding ballast tanks and supplying water to sanitary and fire pumps; also as a boiler blow down.

sextant: An instrument used in measuring the angular distance between objects, used chiefly by navigators in determining position by measurement of the angle between a heavenly body and the horizon.

spectacle irons: A three-ring iron attached to the clew of a square sail through which three lines can be hooked, tack, sheet and clew garnet.

shackles: Any variety of connecting devices, most often roughly U-shaped, with a pin across the opening.

sheer, sheerline: The longitudinal curve of the rail or decks that shows the variation in height above water or freeboard through the vessel's entire length.

sheet: A line or chain attached to a lower corner of a sail; it is shortened or slackened to control the set of the sail.

shell back: An old, experienced sailor. Anyone who has crossed the equator by ship.

sloop: A small one-masted vessel originally rigged fore and aft with a jib, mainsail, and often topsails and staysails; the modern sloop usually has a jib-headed mainsail and is distinguished from the cutter in having the mast farther forward and only a single headsail.

stern: The after end of a ship or boat.

stateroom: The cabin of an officer other than the captain on a naval vessel.

starboard: The right-hand side of a ship as one faces forward, toward the bow, opposed to *port*.

stays, ship to: When wind is put dead ahead of a sailing vessel, thus stopping the forward motion of vessel.

stern watch: Personnel assigned duty, usually as lookout, at the stern of a vessel.

stop(s) (gasket): A piece of line used in furling sail and keeping it furled.

strip and scuttle: Removal of a ship's gear and sinking of the vessel.

stuffing box: A chamber that holds packing tightly around a moving part, as a piston rod, boat propellor shaft, etc., to prevent leakage of fluid along the part.

tack (tack ship): To turn a sailing craft "through the wind" to take the wind on her other side.

tackle: A combination of a line of blocks working together to assist in lifting or controlling heavy objects on board ship.

taffrail: The rail around the stern of a ship.

talker: A sound-powered phone talker; *e.g.*, assigned to communicate from fo'c'sle lookout station to bridge.

tall ship: Contemporary term for any large sailing vessel, especially square-rigged vessels.

tankage: The storage of fluids, gases, etc., in tanks.

taps: A pipe or bugle call or drum signal to put out lights in retiring for the night. Also sounded at the burial of a soldier or sailor.

thimble: A heart-shaped or round-grooved metal ring inserted into a loop of line or in the eye of a splice, to prevent wear.

tidal berth: A berth or dock in an open harbor that allows a ship to remain afloat in any tide while alongside.

tops: Platforms at the heads of the lower masts of sailing ships.

topside: The part of a ship's side above the waterline.

track (well): A course or line of motion or action; route; way.

transom: Any of the transverse beams attached to the sternpost of a wooden ship. The upper outside portion of a ship's stern.

transverse framing: In ship construction, a system of framing in which closely spaced frames of similar scantlings are used to provide the main strength framing of the ship, upon which the shell, keel, and decks are attached; in contradistinction to longitudinal framing, in which many closely spaced longitudinals are used, with greater frame spacing, lighter frames, and occasional web frames.

trim ballast: Ballast used in the lower bilges of a ship to set the ship "on her lines."

turnbuckles: Adjustable screw fittings designed to adjust the tension of standing rigging.

vang: A piece of running rigging employed at the ends of spars to prevent them, especially gaffs, from "sagging" too far to leeward.

waist deck: The central portion of the main weather deck. On board *Eagle* and most square-riggers, located between the raised fore and after decks.

warping to: Cables to move a vessel from one place to another in a port, river, or harbor by means of warps (lines) fastened to buoys, anchors, or some fixed object ashore.

warrant officer: An ex–enlisted hand who professionally has attained officer status and is at the peak of his rating specialty.

watch duty (detail): The specific personnel designated to stand a watch.

watchstander: Personnel who are on watch.

waterline: That position along a ship's hull where vessel and water meet, loaded or unloaded, and on an even keel.

wharf: A structure of wood or stone, sometimes roofed over, built at the shore of a harbor, river, etc., for ships to lie alongside, as during loading or unloading; pier; dock.

wheel (also: helm): Steering wheel.

winch: Any of various devices operated by crank or power; specifically, a type of windlass for hoisting or hauling, having a crank connected by gears to a horizontal drum around which the rope or chain is wound.

windage: The part of a ship's surface exposed to wind.

wind-heel criteria: Standards for ship stability under varying forces.

windward: The direction or side from which the wind blows; it is a point of reference in designating a movement or a location.

wings: Deck areas on either side of the bridge.

wormed, served, and parceled: A system of protecting cabled standing rigging from weathering and corrosion. Collectively called "service."

yard(s): A slender rod or spar, tapering toward the ends, fastened at right angles across a mast to support a sail.

zooplankton: Very small, often microscopic animals that live in the upper oceanic water. Along with phytoplankton (plants), they constitute the bottom of the oceanic food chain.

Bibliography

Chapelle, Howard I., *The History of the American Sailing Navy*. New York: W. W. Norton, 1949.

———,*The History of American Sailing Ships*. New York: W. W. Norton, 1935.

Earle, Captain William, "A Midlife Evaluation of *Eagle*." U.S.C.G. Academy *Bulletin*, Sept.–Oct., 1983.

King, Irving H., *George Washington's Coast Guard*. Annapolis: Naval Institute, 1978.

McGowan, Captain Gordon P., *The Eagle and the Skipper*. New York: Van Nostrand, 1960.

Norton, William I., *Eagle Ventures*. New York: M. Evans and Co., 1970.

Regan, Cmdr. Paul N., *Eagle Seamanship* with an introduction by Paul Johnson. Annapolis: Naval Institute, 1979.

Underhill, Harold A., *Masting and Rigging the Clipper Ship & Ocean Carrier*. Glasgow: Brown, Son & Ferguson, 1946.

———, *Sail Training and Cadet Ships*. Glasgow: Brown, Son & Ferguson, 1955.

Villiers, Alan, *Sailing Eagle*. New York: Charles Scribner's Sons, 1955.

———,"Under Canvas in the Atomic Age," *National Geographic*, July 1955.

Index

Page numbers in italics indicate an illustration or photograph.